Welcome to the Wonderful World of Wicketkeepers

Also by Luke Sutton

The Life of a Sports Agent: The Middleman
(White Owl, 2020)

Back from the Edge: Mental Health and Addiction in Sport
(White Owl, 2019)

Welcome to the Wonderful World of Wicketkeepers

Luke Sutton

WHITE OWL

AN IMPRINT OF PEN & SWORD BOOKS LTD.
YORKSHIRE – PHILADELPHIA

First published in Great Britain in 2022 by
Pen & Sword White Owl
An imprint of
Pen & Sword Books Ltd
Yorkshire - Philadelphia

ISBN 978 1 52678 478 0

Printed and bound by CPI Group (UK) Ltd, Croydon CR0 4YY

Pen & Sword Books Ltd. incorporates the Imprints of Pen & Sword
Archaeology, Atlas, Aviation, Battleground, Discovery, Family History, History,
Maritime, Military, Naval, Politics, Railways, Select, Transport, True Crime,
Fiction, Frontline Books, Leo Cooper, Praetorian Press, Seaforth Publishing,
Wharncliffe and White Owl.

For a complete list of Pen & Sword titles please contact

PEN & SWORD BOOKS LIMITED
47 Church Street, Barnsley, South Yorkshire, S70 2AS, England
E-mail: enquiries@pen-and-sword.co.uk
Website: www.pen-and-sword.co.uk

or

PEN AND SWORD BOOKS
1950 Lawrence Rd, Havertown, PA 19083, USA
E-mail: uspen-and-sword@casematepublishers.com
Website: www.penandswordbooks.com

This book is dedicated to anyone who gets the gloves on and throws themselves into wicketkeeping.
You are all bloody heroes of the game!

Contents

Foreword

A man who works with his hands is a labourer; a man who works with his hands and his brain is a craftsman; but a man who works with his hands and his brain and his heart is an artist.

Louis Nizer

Wicketkeeping is one of the great arts of cricket on which everyone apparently has an opinion and yet few really know what they are talking about. Wicketkeepers are one of a kind in cricket teams and often one of a kind in life as well. Almost all my life has been spent in or around wicketkeeping and this book reflects my deep passion for it. I wanted to put something into the world that helped lift the lid on what the world of a wicketkeeper is truly like and why there are so many misconceptions about it.

Any time someone takes up the position of wicketkeeper within a team it is something special. There is just one of you, and for as long as you hold the gloves in that team, at whatever level, you have a huge responsibility within it. The history of cricket will always hold 'keepers' in great reverence because of the importance and unique nature of the position.

This book is a celebration of wicketkeepers that is led by wicketkeepers themselves. Above all else, I hope it will make cricket lovers smile and have a greater understanding and respect for wicketkeepers. Cricket is a beautiful game, with a plethora of intricacies and mysteries, and wicketkeepers have a role in more of those than anyone else in the team. So, without a true understanding of wicketkeepers, can we really understand the game of cricket?

Chapter 1

There is Only One Wicketkeeper!

I had just finished two school terms in my first year at Millfield Junior School in Somerset, or Edgarley Hall, as it was called then. I was 10 years old and up till then most of my life had been spent in Peru and Holland. And the vast majority of my time in those countries had been taken up with swimming competitively, either in training or competitions – which I absolutely loved.

Millfield was a whole new world for me compared to the dusty and rugged Peru and flat, open spaces of colourful Holland. The swimming programme at the school was exceptional, but they also opened me up to so many other sports that I had either zero or limited knowledge of up to that point in my life. The first term had been rugby and hockey, which were brand new to me, and the second term was hockey and football, the latter of which I'd had some experience of playing before. As I started my third and final term of the school year, the options were athletics and … cricket.

One of my previous teachers in Holland had talked to the whole class about cricket. He was English and loved the sport and wanted us all to know about it. I think he showed us an old video of him playing and we tried to play some sort of game in the playground. But as for my background knowledge of the sport, that was about it. Nonetheless, what the first two terms at Millfield had proved was that I was an all-round sports lover and seemed to be reasonably talented. The intensity of my competitiveness was there for all to see, so the chances of me throwing myself into cricket were high.

In our very first cricket session, our Under-10s cricket master, who also happened to be the school reverend, sat all the boys down who had signed up for cricket to talk through our season ahead. He recognised that there were boys like me who had never played the game seriously before, so he carefully explained that in a cricket team everyone would bat, some would bowl, and one person would be the wicketkeeper. That last bit caught my attention – just one person would be wicketkeeper?

'That's pretty cool,' I thought. Basically, like the goalkeeper in football.

To be clear, at this point I had no idea what the wicketkeeper did. My best guess was that he defended something, like a 'keeper' would do.

'Is there anyone here who would like to be a wicketkeeper?' our cricket master asked.

No one put their hand up.

'No one here fancy trying it?' we were pressed again.

Silence.

And then it dawned on me … there is only one wicketkeeper in a team so if I volunteer for whatever this position is then I am guaranteed a place in the team. Genius!

'I'll do it,' I quickly jumped in, before anyone else could rethink their decision.

'Great! Luke, you are our wicketkeeper!'

For a highly competitive 10-year-old boy, this was a brilliant result. I was now officially in the Edgarley Hall Under-10s

Cricket Team and I was the 'wicketkeeper', no less! There was now just the small matter of finding out what the role involved.

I was soon to discover that the basics of wicketkeeping included catching, jumping around, and essentially being the centre of attention – it was like my dream job! I immediately fell in love and from there began a lifelong fascination with wicketkeeping – the technique, the gloves, the mentality and, yes, the art of it. I threw myself into it and seemed to be pretty good at it early on. I don't really have any strong basis for that assumption other than that I kept being asked do it and eventually became the wicketkeeper for the Somerset Under-10s, Under-11s and so on. Most importantly, I really enjoyed it. I wanted to play as much cricket as possible, and saw myself as a wicketkeeper through and through. When speaking to the various wicketkeepers covered in this book, I discovered that many of them had an early dabble with trying to be a bowler. That wasn't the case for me. I never much enjoyed bowling or felt any inclination to step away from the gloves for it. From day 1 of my cricket life, I was a wicketkeeper.

As my cricket progressed at school and within the Somerset junior levels, my dad took me to my first-ever Test match, when I was 13 years old. It was at Lord's in 1990, with India as the opposition. We sat at the bottom of the Grace Stand and watched Graham Gooch bat incredibly in scoring his infamous 333. I will never forget watching Gooch so effortlessly hit the Indian leg-spinner Narendra Hirwani for six into the Nursery End. From where we sat in the Grace Stand, it looked like the ball was travelling into space. I also remember the power of Robin Smith's cut shot – like a bullet off the bat! We only watched England bat, but I was so captivated by it all that my dad kindly took me to the third Test at The Oval in the same series. In that Test, I recall watching Michael Atherton bowl some suspicious leg spin but what I remember most is Jack Russell's wicketkeeping. He was brilliant and so unique. The ball seemed to melt into his gloves, and he made everything look so easy. For such a small man, he seemed to command great attention on the field. But, more than anything else, there seemed to be a rhythm to what he was doing. It was like there was a gentle drumbeat going on somewhere in the background and every movement he made was in sync with it. He never expended too much energy, but it was always just enough. I will never forget watching Jack and thinking that the skill he was showing us was a thing of beauty.

From that moment in my life, I watched Jack and his Australian counterpart, Ian Healy, keep wicket as much as possible on television. I loved Jack's old gloves – like huge pieces of black meat that swallowed the ball into an abyss. Equally, I loved everything about Healy – he was immaculate, the epitome of precision. He shared that beautiful rhythm to his wicketkeeping that Jack had, like he was born to be a wicketkeeper. They were so different and yet both embodied everything I perceived a wicketkeeper to be – they were leaders, master craftsmen and individuals. I was enthralled by them.

As my cricket progressed, I was fortunate to start being picked for the England junior squads, which would involve training camps at Lilleshall in Shropshire. During these camps, I was even more fortunate to have been coached by the great Alan Knott. My experience with Alan only enhanced my fascination with wicketkeeping. Alan was truly ahead of his time as a coach; he was simply outstanding. He used video analysis with his own makeshift VCR set up and treated wicketkeeping as an obsession that could only inspire you. I don't think I ever walked away from a session with him without feeling 100 per cent improved. Alan had this beautiful balance in showing you how you needed to improve while boosting your confidence exponentially. As with every great coach I have worked with, Alan's desire to simply make you better, without any other agenda, was unquestionable. During your sessions with him, you knew that he was laser focused on improving you as a wicketkeeper and that was it. It was with Alan that, among many things, I actually learned the skill of diving. That might sound odd to many of you – 'Surely a dive is just a dive,' you might think. However, that's not the case. There is a definite skill to it. In fact, the entire movement suddenly became smooth to me. Something that was so based on power swiftly became graceful. I would then watch Jack take a diving catch on the television and see that exact skill executed as Alan and I had practised.

Importantly, Alan helped me to see that we wicketkeepers were in our own little community. Yes, bowlers and batsmen had their own groups, but it was on another level with us 'keepers'. We were seen as different, and the truth is that we *were* different. During our lunch breaks at the England camps at Lilleshall, I would watch as everyone walked off to the dining hall and yet Alan would stay behind and open his home-made sandwiches. He didn't need to be with everyone else; he was very happy in his own company, being what some people would see as a little 'different'. You could never accuse him of being anti-social, but he was very comfortable being an individual. I was as absorbed in him as I was in watching Jack and Healy on TV.

It was during this time in my life when the debate began between whether England should select Alec Stewart over

Jack Russell to keep wicket. Stewart was a cricketer I rated enormously. I admired his batting style from deep in the crease and how he always 'fronted up' to the opposition. In the heat of the battle, he took people on rather than wilted away – I loved that. This might sound strange but that punchy nature to Stewart's cricket felt quite un-English at the time. Particularly in the Ashes, we seemed to be fairly gracious losers in the face of Aussie in-your-face aggression. Stewart was different in this respect. He seemed to enjoy taking people on and, in the process, annoying them. To this day, I am still a little bit in awe of him when I talk to him – Stewart is a proper England legend. So, I felt a bit conflicted in the debate between him and Jack as wicketkeeper. I absolutely understood the argument to play Stewart as the wicketkeeper and free up another spot for a batsman or bowler in the team. It made sense, *but* Jack was Jack! It was hard to ever consider that Jack Russell would *not* be the England wicketkeeper! However, what happened during this debate was that it made me think about the wicketkeeper's role in a way that I hadn't before. Up to that point, I had placed wicketkeeping as an art form that only the best of the best were allowed to touch for England and now it felt like we were considering making it a less specialist position. Of course, with the benefit of hindsight I now realise that this was absolutely the right debate to have, but at the time it was a difficult one to compute in my head. I would just like to add that Stewart was an outstanding wicketkeeper for England. I don't want this talking point to undermine his performances for England, because he was brilliant. I think Stewart would agree that Jack was a superior wicketkeeper but that doesn't mean that he didn't reach the highest standards with the gloves.

As the Stewart/Russell debate raged on in my own head as well as in the heads of every other cricket fan, it made me realise how opinionated people were about wicketkeepers. There was only one of us in a team, yet it felt like every man and his dog had their say on the wicketkeeper: to be blunt, everyone thought they were a bloody expert! I heard Stewart criticised for things that I felt were very harsh or simply wrong, and people even began to question Jack's style. It was perplexing. I started to see the comparison with how we dealt with football goalkeepers equally harshly. I didn't mind the criticism I heard dished out when it was fair but more often than not it was said from a position of naïvety. I just didn't see that happening for batsmen and bowlers.

I also started to notice the constant comparison to wicketkeepers of 'yesteryear' as commentators and pundits pontificated over how the current lot compared with Alan Knott and Bob Taylor. Yet wicketkeeping was evolving rapidly – Healy was entirely different to Jack in technique, gloves and style, but they were both brilliant. Wicketkeepers were popping up all over county and international cricket with hybrid techniques of Healy and Russell, or something entirely different. Someone I will talk about more, Karl Krikken at Derbyshire, had a technique that was completely his own, but as Alan Knott used to say to me, 'The most important thing is that you catch the ball.' It was like we had opened up Pandora's Box for the masses to comment on the beautiful art of wicketkeeping and we were feeling the consequences. It felt to me like we had lots of batsmen and bowlers trying to talk about something they weren't that up to speed on and the best idea was to think back to how Knott and Taylor made them feel. Please remember that this was my experience of this – I don't doubt it wasn't the first time that it had happened in the history of the game, it was just the first time that I had experienced it.

I was reminded of this during Bobby Bracey's debut for England at Lord's against New Zealand. A debut is an extremely nervy occasion for any cricketer, especially at Lord's, and it can be a tricky place to keep wicket on the first day. Yet, only at lunchtime on day 1 of the match, Mike Selvey, an ex-fast bowler and now journalist, tweeted: 'Early observation is that Bracey is a pretty average keeper. Not bad but far from exceptional.'

Bracey had been keeping for two hours for England and yet he had already been dealt this fairly damning assessment of his abilities. We couldn't even let him have the whole first innings before he was given his verdict; instead, we took the first two nervy hours of his international cricket career to do so. It is crazy. Bracey went on to have a couple of difficult Test matches with the gloves but that's not the point. What is the rush for us to give an assessment on a wicketkeeper? Do we do this to batsmen and bowlers? The answer to that last question is a firm no. We have learned from our lessons of the 'One-Test Wonders' during the 1990s that we need to give players a fair amount of time to show themselves on the international stage, yet the same approach doesn't always seem to apply to wicketkeepers.

I continued to follow the world of wicketkeepers intently throughout my teenage years and was eventually fortunate enough to be offered a contract and become a professional wicketkeeper for Somerset CCC. As many of you know, this then became my career for over fifteen years, during which I kept wicket to the likes of Muttiah Muralitharan, Jimmy Anderson and many other exceptional bowlers. My fascination with the role became my reality, my job. I experienced everything a wicketkeeper can, from feeling brilliant to having major crises in confidence. I played through broken and dislocated fingers, and tinkered with my technique all the time. I heard criticism and praise – maybe the former a little more than the latter! I lived as a wicketkeeper and loved it. Throughout it all, I learned that the game of cricket does not ever slow down for you as a wicketkeeper. Whatever you are feeling at whatever time, the game will always demand the same from the wicketkeeper; it will not make allowances for you. If you are a bowler and are not asked to bowl by the captain, or a batsman watching the guys in the middle smash it around, then you can have some 'downtime' in your role. This doesn't exist when it is your time to be a wicketkeeper during a game. In fact, at the professional level this is ramped up even more if you have an injury. You simply can't walk off the field, because you are a specialist and the team need you to do your job. Nine hundred and ninety-nine times out of a thousand, you have to grit your teeth and simply get on with it. My former coach at Derbyshire, Dave Houghton, pointed this out to me when I said that I would play in a game with a broken finger.

'That's great, but just know that this game won't fucking care that you have a broken finger.'

And he was 100 per cent correct.

Despite now being retired and never actually wanting to keep wicket ever again due to how old I feel, I am still in love with it. I am as fascinated with the art of wicketkeeping as ever. There is a depth to the complexities of wicketkeeping that I don't think many cricket fans understand or have ever had explained to them. The wicketkeeping community includes such a broad range of personalities and techniques that it can include what appear to be polar opposites, such as in Jack Russell and

Alec Stewart. In the modern game, we can look at Ben Foakes versus Jos Buttler and judge one as a 'proper keeper' and the other as not so much – yet they are both excellent and part of the same family within cricket. A lot of this comes from not truly understanding wicketkeeping and hearing comments and judgements made by people who may sound like they know what they are talking about but really don't. So, I decided to try to do something about this.

I wanted to combine my love of wicketkeeping with my newfound love of writing and put together something that was very different for this unique and wonderful role in cricket. My challenge was to give people an insight into wicketkeeping and wicketkeepers that they might not have seen before. I wanted to help people look beyond lazy analysis and get inside the heads of the brilliant people actually doing the job. Importantly, I wanted this to be fun and flow with some humour and fascinating insight rather than getting bogged down in technical points. One thing the wicketkeeping fraternity has is characters, and interwoven into their eccentricity is brilliance – there really can be method in the madness! Lastly, I wanted to dig into what mindset it takes to do the job successfully for years and years when at times it can be an extremely lonely and thankless task.

Do wicketkeepers themselves really know what makes them survive and thrive? How do they see themselves as personalities and cricketers? How do they view their counterparts? What are the craziest things they have ever thought or been told about wicketkeeping? Do you need to be eccentric like Jack or tidy and clean like Stewart? Are you really the 'drummer in the band', as wicketkeepers are often described in a cricket team? There were many questions that I wanted to dig into.

I think wicketkeeping is the best job in cricket and everyone who does it is a bloody hero. My son recently told me that he would like to do more wicketkeeping, and I can honestly say that I have never pushed him towards it. The hours we have shared down at the nets practising have been wonderful. It has brought back to me my early experiences of being coached when I thought there wasn't much to wicketkeeping but was then opened up to this huge cupboard of knowledge and technique. People who love cricket often fall in love with its intricacies – the more they know, the more they want to know. Well, I don't think wicketkeeping is any different. It is a treasure trove of information and mystery. When you start tapping into it, you want to know everything. It is truly wonderful.

The final point I want to make in this opening chapter is that I wanted this book to be led by the wicketkeepers who I interviewed. I wanted them to tell the story of what it is like being a wicketkeeper through their very own experiences. I was extremely lucky have the opportunity to speak to some of the very best this country has ever produced, and without them this book wouldn't be what it is. The group included a broad range of wicketkeepers so that we could get as rounded an insight as possible. They were all brilliant, and I thank them all so much for their honesty and candour.

Chapter 2

Perception is Everything

When I started my professional cricket career at Somerset CCC, the wicketkeeper ahead of me was Rob Turner.

Rob was a brilliant performer with bat and gloves for Somerset and, in truth, a long way ahead of me. During my final season with the county in 1999, Rob was really pushing for England honours. He was selected for England A winter tour (now the England Lions) and was definitely competing amongst the best wicketkeeper-batsmen in the country. The interesting thing for me was that Rob didn't look how most wicketkeepers were perceived to look like at that time. He was comfortably over 6 feet tall and stood in a very different wicketkeeping stance while waiting for the ball than the likes of Jack Russell, Warren Hegg, Richard Blakey, Chris Read, Steven Rhodes and Keith Piper – with whom he was competing at the time. He didn't crouch down in a low posture and would often have his hands apart before bringing them together to catch the ball, which was a big no-no at that time in wicketkeeping coaching circles. Ironically, Rob's technique had a lot of similarities with that of Ben Foakes today, but back then, he looked 'different'.

Rob was competing during a time when it was universally recognised that wicketkeepers needed to offer more than just a little to the team as a batsman, and he definitely did that. In that 1999 season he averaged over 50 with the bat as well as keeping brilliantly, yet there seemed a reluctance to pick him. Did that reluctance come from how he looked? Well, Rob was another challenge to what we believed wicketkeepers should look like back then. It felt like we had got to the point where we could stomach an Alec Stewart keeping ahead of Jack Russell, but just not yet, to the point where we could pick a guy who was over 6 feet tall and didn't look anything like any of his counterparts. Rob was also really 'normal' – a well-spoken Cambridge graduate who hardly fell into the eccentric wicketkeeper category. I felt in the late 1990s like we were still trying to package everyone into a version of Alan Knott, Bob Taylor or Jack Russell. Rob Turner didn't fit into this.

This range of personality and appearance within the wicketkeeping fraternity is something I find interesting and is often, I feel, the thing that dominates whether a commentator or fan rates someone. Does that wicketkeeper fit within what that person perceives a wicketkeeper should look and act like at that time? I appreciate that technique in cricket is debated constantly in all areas, but we seem to hold a unique space for this in wicketkeeping. This even exists amongst professional cricket squads in which the general knowledge on wicketkeeping is often limited to players saying 'he or she has lovely hands', which means a wicketkeeper appears to catch the ball fairly effortlessly. In truth, I don't see a role in cricket more dominated by perception than wicketkeeping. In what could be considered an easy job to evaluate ('How many balls did he drop during today's play?'), we seemed to find ourselves with mixed and complicated assessments. A good example of this is when I watched Michael Atherton give a wicketkeeping evaluation before the start of play during a Lord's Test match a few years ago. During his feature he made the point that a simply competent catcher could handle being a wicketkeeper standing back to the fast bowlers as it was a relatively easy job. Like probably every other wicketkeeper in England, I shuddered when I heard him say that. Of all cricket grounds, Lord's can be a tough place to keep wicket standing back. The 'wobble' that keepers may experience there can be very difficult to handle. This is where a seemingly normal ball can pass through to you, but on the way, it wobbles as the ball is affected by the general atmosphere. Ask any wicketkeeper and they will tell you what a nightmare this is. Lord's is infamous for it and it is why we so often see overseas wicketkeepers really struggle there in an early season Test match. In recent times, Adam Gilchrist, Brendon McCullum and Mark Boucher have all had this struggle and had to quickly adapt their techniques to better cope with it. Nonetheless, here was an ex-opening batsman commentating on the difficultly of wicketkeeping in a way that many fans would believe without question. I think that Michael's comments came from his perception of the job having stood at first slip, and comments made by Bob Taylor, who once said:

Standing up to the wicket is what keeping is all about. At first-class level, any competent catcher – a decent slip fielder – can put the gloves on, like Marcus Trescothick, or Graeme Fowler and Graham Gooch when I was playing. They can all keep wicket to a degree. But up to the stumps sorts the men out from the boys. That's where you can see a true wicketkeeper.

I simply think that there has been a misinterpretation of these comments, which have fed into an existing perception of wicketkeeping. Taylor has never said that standing back is easy;

his point was more about how you separate the outstanding wicketkeepers from the average ones, and that is by judging them on their ability to stand up to the wicket. I discuss this point further in my chapter with Chris Read.

So, without meaning to be disrespectful to Atherton, of whom I am massive fan, his perception of wicketkeeping is unfortunately not based on facts. We only needed to ask any of the high-class international wicketkeepers that I have already mentioned or any other England wicketkeeper of recent times who has struggled with the 'wobbling' ball at Lord's. Interestingly, Atherton, writing in a recent newspaper column, defended Bobby Bracey's performance with the gloves in the two Tests versus New Zealand at the start of the 2021 summer due to, guess what – our perception! In his words:

> Bracey had a difficult, even horrid, introduction to Test cricket. He scored nought, nought and eight and looked out of his depth with the bat. He had two difficult patches as a wicketkeeper: one at Lord's and one at Edgbaston, where the wobbling Dukes ball created some fumbles. He dropped a catch. The numbers suggest a more nuanced story. At Lord's, statistics suggested Bracey caught 98 per cent of balls; at Edgbaston, that fell to 96 per cent. I checked those with CricViz, the analytics company, which had him at 98 per cent and 97 per cent. An overall rate of 97 per cent puts him squarely between county standard (96 per cent) and elite (98 per cent) ... pretty good. My guess is that as many people would be as surprised by those numbers as I was. We all suffer from biases and heuristics. Because

Bracey is an inexperienced keeper, because he does not look like a natural catcher (or mover) and because he is a manufactured batsman-wicketkeeper, the fumbles stay in our mind. They become exaggerated. We forget, perhaps, that one of the most natural wicketkeepers of all, Jack Russell, dropped a catch on his debut (a much easier one, as it happens).

Atherton has, in many ways, made my point for me having said what he said previously about standing back and then writing this reflective piece about our perception of Bracey's performance. In my opinion, individual perception plays a powerful role in the assessment of wicketkeeping.

Part of this perception problem might be a romance that cricket holds for wicketkeepers. They are our mercurial personalities whom we love to reminisce and tell stories about. Maybe the evolution of wicketkeepers away from the mystery and technique of Alan Knott, Bob Taylor and Jack Russell is not necessarily welcomed by some people – because they don't 'look right'. Maybe some don't want our wicketkeepers to be 'normal' in personality, or tall, or anything other than resemble the keepers of yesteryear. Just maybe the stereotypical view of the wicketkeeper is part of the nostalgic beauty we all hold for cricket. I have to admit that I was probably susceptible to that during my career. I loved hearing stories about how brilliantly Alan Knott used to stand up to Derek Underwood on uncovered pitches and felt like his technique might be the only one any of us should have. Likewise, I loved hearing about the eccentricity of wicketkeepers. My teammate at Derbyshire, Dominic Cork, used to regale stories of touring with Jack Russell for England,

and I enjoyed hearing about every detail. When Dominic Hewson joined Derbyshire from Gloucestershire, I was ready and waiting to ask him a multitude of questions about Jack. I was as in love with the persona of the 'keeper' as anyone. So, perhaps we are resistant to changing our image of a wicketkeeper. Is it like a hardened rugby fan wanting their prop forward to be a beer-swilling, red meat-eating nutcase rather than a vegan, yoga-practising academic?

My most significant move in professional cricket could hardly have given me a bigger example of the complexities of how people perceived wicketkeeping. I was desperate to play first team cricket but my chances of breaking through at Somerset were very limited due to the consistent standard that Rob produced. My second team coach at Somerset was Colin Wells, who then became head coach at Derbyshire. He spoke to me and suggested I join him in the midlands because my path to first team cricket could be much faster there. He felt that I had a decent chance of competing to get into Derbyshire's first team as a batsman and that I could eventually challenge Karl Krikken, who was the incumbent wicketkeeper at the time. I had seen Karl, or 'Krik', keep on television, and he looked interesting in every possible way. He had all sorts of strange movements and almost looked like a waiting gorilla leaning on his knuckles when standing up to the stumps. But he was brilliant. He, again, looked different, but was outstanding. His ability in standing up to the stumps to seamers was second to none. What was also clear from watching him on TV was that he was certainly on the more eccentric side of the wicketkeeper range!

I took Colin Wells's advice and headed to Derbyshire in the winter of 1999/2000. Back in those days, winter training programmes were still a work in progress. We reported for a few boxercise sessions at the local David Lloyd Leisure Club but that was about it for the pre-Christmas months. In the main, you were left to your own devices until after Christmas, when cricket would start again. For some reason, my contact with Krik was limited that winter. It might have been that he went away for that time to play overseas. It wasn't until the prospect of our preseason tour to Portugal that the character that was Krik really hit home for me. Details were being released to the players for the tour, which included who was sharing a room with whom. There seemed to be a buzz around who was sharing with Krik.

'Who are you with, Sutts?' I would be asked.

'Krik,' I would reply, and then the giggles would start.

What was clear to me was that sharing a room with Krik on a preseason tour was something other people found hilariously funny when it wasn't them having to do it. I really had no idea what everyone was going on about and would get comments like, 'You'll see', which hardly filled me with serenity about the whole thing.

When we arrived at the resort in Portugal and headed to our rooms, I could only say that Krik seemed like one of the happiest people I had ever met. With his deep Wigan accent, he would joke away, mainly with Dominic Cork. Krik and Dominic were like a double act, constantly ribbing each other for one thing or another. What could possibly be that much to worry about with Krik?

Well, maybe the first warning was when he started to unload the bottles of TCP fluid antiseptic from his bag into our bathroom. I think up to that point in my life, TCP cream had been something that my mum had rubbed on some wound of mine that needed to be clear of infection. I can't say I had ever seen the fluid form used for anything, especially not involving wicketkeepers.

'What's the TCP for, Krik?' I asked.

'Well, my mate, I just use it to keep me all clean and healthy,' he replied in his cheery Wigan accent.

I didn't have a clue what he meant.

It turned out that what Krik meant was that he would snort and gargle TCP every morning! He felt it cleaned his 'insides'. Our room absolutely stank from the pungent smell – it was horrific! There was no escaping the aroma, day or night, and Krik seemed completely oblivious to it. And that wasn't the end of it …

Krik seemed to have lots of Asilone tablets lying around, a medication for indigestion that I had never seen before. He would take an Asilone tablet and wedge it in his top gum at the back of his mouth. I have no idea why he would put such a tablet in his gums but when I asked him, he replied: 'Well, my mate, I sometimes get too much saliva in my mouth, and this really helps dry my mouth out.'

Too much saliva.

It was hard to know what to make of it all. It was one of those weird moments when I couldn't work out whether I was massively missing an obvious trick in life or Krik was wonderfully bonkers. What I did know for sure was that, regardless of what the TCP and Asilone were doing for him, his snoring was on a level that you cannot appreciate by simply reading this. It was INSANE.

I will admit that I can get a snore on at times but listening to Krik snore was like listening to a wild animal – it was extraordinary. On our first night, I had to move into the lounge area in our apartment, which was an improvement, but no bedroom door was going to prevent Krik's snoring breaking through. I considered whether it was causing interference on radar systems around southern Europe. Within twenty-four hours, I entirely understood why my teammates found such entertainment in the fact that the new boy at the club was sharing a room with Krik.

Krik was different in every way possible, but underneath it all, he was a phenomenally good wicketkeeper. I learned a massive amount from him, and he dispelled so many wicketkeeping myths for me. There has always been this idea floating around that wicketkeepers need 'soft hands'. It was alleged than when the likes of Jack Russell or Keith Piper caught the ball, you wouldn't be able to hear it hit their gloves because their hands were so soft. This was to some extent true. Yet Krik was the absolute opposite of this. He actually had what you might describe as 'hard hands' and the ball made a solid thud when he caught it. He was magnificent standing up to the stumps to fast bowlers and there would be absolutely no give in his gloves or body when he caught the ball. If anything, he would slightly attack the ball. What Krik showed me was the importance of holding the line and height of the ball at all times before you caught it. He didn't practise 'soft hands' because he didn't want to be tempted to move off the ball in an attempt to make it go into his gloves more softly.

So, here was Karl Krikken, the stereotypical eccentric wicketkeeper, but in technical terms he was very different to many others of his era, yet still brilliant. He was just another example that in a field of wicketkeeping in which many people wanted to put them in a box conforming to what they considered a keeper should look like, there is enormous variety. To truly understand wicketkeepers is to be able to see that not one size fits all.

However, there is one thing that all wicketkeepers have in common – they never forget their dropped catches. For full transparency, I am actually stealing a comment made by Matt Prior at the end of his career. Dropped catches live long in the memory of each keeper, where they can find themselves in the loneliest place in cricket after this sort of mistake.

I remember dropping Mark Ramprakash at The Oval and he went on to get a hundred. I remember dropping Ian Blackwell at Chester-le-Street and he went on to score a crucial half-century in a low-scoring match that we ended up losing. And to top them all off, I remember dropping Michael Lumb at the Rose Bowl off Dominic Cork, which was hands down the easiest catch I have ever dropped (and no first-class wicketkeeper should ever drop).

You remember them all.

So, whatever your perceptions are of what a wicketkeeper should look and behave like, there is no question that they experience something in their role that is unique within cricket. As the Australian writer Gideon Haigh brilliantly observed about a wicketkeeper waiting for a catch: 'Imagine standing at a bus stop without a timetable, waiting for a bus that may come in a minute or in six hours.' I would add, imagine then dropping that catch. There are few experiences within cricket that can compare to this.

This is what prompted the Indian journalist Suresh Menon to say, 'You don't have to be mad to be a wicketkeeper, but it helps.'

I hope that by now I have made a strong case for you to understand that the wicketkeeping community is a big tent full of personalities and techniques surrounded by the rest of the cricket community opining on what they believe makes a good wicketkeeper! Wicketkeeping will always drive debate because it is a distinctive job done by the smallest number of people in cricket. Therefore, by nature, it will be misunderstood by many.

In my opinion, wicketkeeping truly is an art form. There is a grace and beauty to it when done well that will make people watch in absolute awe, but that doesn't mean everyone has to do it the same way or that everyone who does it brilliantly even has to believe it is an art form. It can be just a job to some people, and that is OK. That doesn't mean they care any less about it or do it any less brilliantly – they just see it differently.

The evolving nature of wicketkeeping challenges people's perceptions of what the job should be like and it will do that many times over. Cricket is a game of bat versus ball and the wicketkeeper will always find themselves stuck in the middle of that battle in how they best fit the team's needs. In recent times, this has only been heightened by the changing formats of the game. As my first cricket master said, every team needs a wicketkeeper, but how we perceive the role of that wicketkeeper can vary enormously. As a result, wicketkeeping will always drive debate.

One dropped catch or missed stumping can dominate the narrative around that keeper regardless of what else they have done that day. In essence, a wicketkeeper is attempting to be 'perfect' every day of their career, which is simply impossible. It is also not what any other cricketing role demands. A bowler doesn't start the day expecting of themselves to bowl every ball perfectly, nor a batsman to play every shot without fault; but the expectation around a wicketkeeper is different.

The people to whom we should listen about wicketkeeping are the keepers themselves. They are the heroes of the history of this role in cricket. They have lived, breathed and felt every ounce of what being a wicketkeeper is all about. They can let us into a world that others just presume to know about.

Welcome to the Wonderful World of Wicketkeepers.

Chapter 3

Jos Buttler

2010 was a year of crossroads for me and Jos Buttler.
Craig Kieswetter had secured a regular place in the England One Day International side and went on to win the T20 World Cup later that year. Kieswetter's progress on the international stage meant that Jos would get an extended run in the Somerset first team as a wicketkeeper-batsman. It was a year when Jos would start to register on everyone's radar as a highly talented all-round cricketer.

For me, well, maybe 2010 could have been described as the absolute opposite – the beginning of the end for my professional cricketer career. As I went into that season at Lancashire, I was under increasing pressure to perform, and I was well aware of it. I was turning 34 that year and, if I am honest, I wasn't getting any better as a player. Peter Moores was my head coach and had always backed me, but I knew I needed to repay that. In an early May County Championship match at Old Trafford against Somerset, I took a step towards doing that. It was a match in which Jos played and kept wicket and I managed to score 118 opening the batting. It could well have been one of the best innings of my career against a very handy Somerset seam bowling attack. It was an innings in which I managed to score eighteen boundaries. I will repeat that for anyone familiar with my dogged batting style – YES, eighteen boundaries! I even surprised myself. It was one of those rare innings where, after a slow start, I felt in complete control; in total contrast to 99.9 per cent of my career, I felt like I could hit fours. As my innings went on, I just didn't feel like I was going to get out. That was until Zander de Bruyn got one to bounce a little bit more and I gloved it down the leg side. It was a healthy piece of glove so initially I felt like it could be another boundary. As I jerked my head around to see where the ball was going, I looked behind and saw Jos take an incredible one-handed catch down the leg side. I remember seeing the ball sweetly hit the middle of his glove without the slightest doubt that it would pop out. By any standards, it was a very fine catch. I believe the match was the first time I had ever watched Jos keep wicket and that catch registered firmly in my memory.

Later that season, when my performances had started to significantly wane, we played a forty-over match at Taunton. If ever a match summed up the two different places mine and Jos's careers were at, this was it. Somerset batted first and Jos came in at number 6 and scored 64 not out off thirty-seven balls, with seven fours and two sixes. I recall watching his style of hitting and feeling like there was almost a hockey technique to it where his wrists snapped across the ball so sharply and with incredible power. More distinctly, I remember thinking as I stood behind the stumps that what Jos was doing with the bat was something that in my wildest dreams I couldn't do. And to almost emphasise this point to the cricketing gods, when it was my turn to bat, I scored 9 off twenty-two balls in a miserable loss. It was painful!

Craig Kieswetter was actually keeping wicket in that game, and as I came in to bat, he gave me a little chirp from behind the stumps: 'Here come some tired legs.'

As he made the comment, I actually chuckled to myself. He was 100 per cent right – I had tired legs and a tired mind to go with it.

This match was like the old meeting the new. The white ball game in England was moving forward at an alarming rate with the likes of Jos and I just didn't have the skills to keep up. And right there and then, in the middle of the Taunton pitch under floodlights, with Craig Kieswetter chirping away at me, I bloody knew it – I was tired. In fact, I had never felt older in a cricketing sense. What the likes of Jos were bringing to the game ushered in a whole new era. They were making the impossible seem very possible. They were realigning all the batting 'rules' that had existed up till then. Needing 6, 7 or even 8 an over was now a breeze. Hitting the balls 360 degrees around the ground was now entirely doable. The norms were being rewritten and the old, including me, were being left behind.

I remember the buzz around the ground as Jos batted that day. The players on the balcony and the crowd all knew what a special talent this guy was. There was an air of anticipation as he took strike – it felt like anything was possible. And since then, Jos has gone on to show off his special talents on the biggest cricketing stages in the world. He has stunned cricket fans so often that nothing seems a lost cause until Jos has had his say in a match. This is nicely summed up when England are in difficulty and Jos walks out to bat, and the cricket journalist, George Dobell, always tweets: 'Hey, Jos, can you do that thing where you turn water into wine, please?' That is the reputation Jos has built for himself, which is why it was even more remarkable that when we chatted together for this chapter, he couldn't have come across as any more unassuming. In hearing his humility and gentle manner, you could be forgiven for forgetting that he is one of the most talented cricketers England have ever produced. This was beautifully summed up when I asked him what he most loved about wicketkeeping and he told me:

> You've got the best view of what's happening ... sometimes I am stood behind batters and thinking this guy is actually taking the Mick now. How can they be operating at that level? De Villiers, especially against spin, there are times when he looks like he's shaping up for something and then suddenly jumps out and plays a different shot, and I can't see how he can do that.

After Jos finished saying this, I had to gently point out to him that that is how we all felt when we watched him bat.

But the point of our hour together was for me to understand him more as a wicketkeeper and, in some ways, I felt like this was going to be one of the more fascinating chats I would have. I suspected I would find out a lot from someone who doesn't necessarily see himself as a traditional keeper. There might be more to discover from someone like Jos, who has had to develop significantly in this role to survive at the highest level.

> No, I certainly wouldn't say I'm a 'keepers' keeper'. This is not to say that I'm not 100 per cent interested in wicketkeeping, but if I turned up to practice and I could only do one thing then I'd probably bat and back myself to be able to keep. I wouldn't say I'm in the boat of the likes of Jack Russell and James Foster, but I really enjoy

the role. I've worked hard on it, tried to get the best out of my ability, but I've always been more of a batter.

With the romanticism that some hold for the role of the wicketkeeper, this honesty from Jos might make them baulk as they want all their keepers to look and sound like Jack Russell and Co. – they want them to *be* keepers! However, this misses a huge point for me. At the time of our chat, it was widely acknowledged that Jos's wicketkeeping had been excellent on the recent tours to Sri Lanka and India, which are two notoriously difficult places to keep wicket. It was evident that Jos had put an enormous amount of time into practice and his keeping was of the highest quality. With the evolution of the wicketkeeper's role, many people have failed to see that just because a player doesn't see themselves as the archetypal 'keeper', that doesn't mean that they are any less committed and cannot continue to perform brilliantly. It simply challenges some of the old-school romantic notions that wicketkeepers need to live and breathe the role, sleep with their gloves on, use the same kit forever and have countless eccentricities! On that point, Jos added:

I'd say most of the guys I was exposed to as wicketkeepers at the start were just not like that. In the England Under-19s, Michael Bates was the keeper and one of the best keepers I have ever seen, for that matter. He was a proper keeper. But he was still very clean and correct. There was no off-the-scale wacky stuff. He was prim and proper, and his kit was always clean. And at Somerset, Craig Kieswetter was the wicketkeeper, and he was also a very clean guy. He always wanted new kit to use. I would hear about keepers who would have gloves for ten years, but Craig would walk out with a brand-new pair of gloves that he's just taken out the wrapper. So, these were the guys that I was exposed to early on and I guess influenced me. It was only when I came across Bruce French that I was introduced to the wacky side of wicketkeeping!

Speaking to Jos reminded me that wicketkeepers are very much influenced by their early counterparts and who they admire within their circle of reach, rather than by any ancient history of the role. That was true for me, even though I was obsessed by Jack Russell. I started standing up to the stumps to seam bowlers because I had seen Toby Bailey do it when we were competing for an England U-15s spot, rather than because I had seen Jack stump Dean Jones off Gladstone Small on TV. Jos did also say how his father had always encouraged him to watch Keith Piper, who made wicketkeeping look so easy. What was crystal clear from speaking to Jos was that although he didn't see himself as a 'keepers' keeper', he had an enormous admiration and interest in other wicketkeepers, including his England rival.

I think Foakesy is an incredible wicketkeeper and I like the fact that he's quite a tall guy. A lot of wicketkeepers are generally quite small, so I love watching his style. His head and hands work so well together. But what I do think about the best wicketkeepers, like Dhoni, is that when they are up to the stumps, they just know what's going to happen before it's happened. It's like they get a sixth sense that this will be the ball that skids on or this is the time that the batsman is going to drag their foot. They just have this incredible awareness that I'm not sure if it comes with experience because I don't think you can teach it. We talk about posture, head and hands and can go down quite a technical rabbit hole with wicketkeeping, but the actual instinct to remain calm when the chance comes is very special.

That is everything that Dhoni is and I love his persona behind the stumps. He's so cool and relaxed, almost like he doesn't care. Ben Scott was like that as well. I loved watching him when he was on the TV and played against him a couple of times. Again, it was like he didn't care and was having a laugh, and yet everything was brilliant.

Jos openly admits that wicketkeeping is not a deep passion for him as it might be for the more traditional wicketkeepers that we have mentioned previously, yet he talks with real depth about what he sees as the mindset of great keepers. Whereas some focus on the technique and eccentricity of great keepers, Jos gravitates towards the ones with the style and mindset he admires. Interestingly, Dhoni was a keeper criticised in the early years of his career. He struggled badly standing back in one tour of England and many labelled him as 'more of a batsman'. He seemed to move slower than some of the keepers we were used to and was another challenge to our perception of a top wicketkeeper. However, through the middle and end of his career, Dhoni was outstanding with gloves, particularly standing up.

It is clear that Jos's evolution as a wicketkeeper has been led by his work on the mindset of the role. I believe that has applied to his batting as well. For guys with his level of natural ability, we sometimes underestimate how much they need to work on their mind. This can especially be the case with someone who looks as calm and collected as Jos does. I really wanted to explore this with him and asked him how it felt when he was keeping well.

> I feel like I'm in a flow. It's like I'm in tune with everything. Timing is a big one for me. You're picking up the cues at the right time and your movements are perfectly timed. I am always really engrossed in the game and everything is working in harmony – you're catching the ball, talking to the guys, giving advice to the bowlers, to the captain and you feel like you're reading the batter. Everything just seems to be in a big package when you're feeling in that flow. I'm not overthinking anything.

From my view of Jos as a keeper, I feel like something mentally had shifted for him in recent times. He seems to have a nice rhythm to his work behind the stumps. I wondered if he had been able to bring something over from his batting mentality to his wicketkeeping. I began by asking him about how it feels when he made a mistake.

> It makes me feel tense even discussing it! It's a horrible place to be, you have nowhere to hide. You drop a catch; you can't slope off to fine leg and hide for a bit. It suddenly becomes very lonely and insular. I feel tension creep down my arms when it happens, and that tension then makes it so hard to keep wicket. And the really hard

thing to remember is that most people have no idea what it's like to be a wicketkeeper. They see us with our gloves and expect us to catch every catch. The majority of the people in the media are not wicketkeepers so they only see a missed stumping rather than an incredibly tough stumping chance. It is a really lonely place to be and your mind can catastrophise everything.

What was most fascinating within this exchange was that Jos quickly moved on to how he has found a way to progress beyond that feeling after making a mistake. He pointed out that all wicketkeepers make mistakes – obviously, the best make the least; but everyone makes mistakes and that is absolutely true. But he has found a way to free himself from the torture of a dropped catch or missed stumping.

One of the biggest skills that the best wicketkeepers have is how quickly they can recover from a mistake and get back that mindset and that mental strength to go, 'OK, that's happened but how can I get back to being in that flow and not let the mistake hang over me?' You have to remember that you might drop a chance at the first session of the first day and you might still have another 150 overs to keep wicket. You must find a way to bring yourself back to a place where you can perform. I have definitely got better at it and it has come from my exploration of psychology and how I can be in the best mental state with both my batting and wicketkeeping – essentially, how I can stay in control of my emotions. What I have realised is that I have a choice. I can feel sorry for myself and allow it to really affect me, or I can choose to try to make the best of that situation. It's impossible to change what's happened if you've made a mistake but I can choose to accept it. I can choose to try and improve. I can choose to still be in a good place and not carry the baggage of it. I really think that's a big one for wicketkeeping to try not to carry a mistake with you. However long it takes, you have got to find a way to get rid of it.

One thing that has certainly helped me in the last few months and years is when something bad happens, we often assume that the same might happen in the next match or a similar mistake might happen. Bad form leads to more bad form. I just flip that. Actually, after a mistake could be the time that something great happens. Why can't the next time be the game where you take the most amazing catch or the best stumping of your life? It doesn't always have to be a bad thing that happens next. This is a mindset that I can choose to have.

It was amazing to listen to Jos talk this through. Such a simple switch in mindset can seem so difficult in times of negativity, but when he breaks it down you can understand that it is an obvious choice for a wicketkeeper when dealing with a mistake.

The number of times Jos referred to being in a flow while wicketkeeping was noteworthy: he clearly places a huge importance on not overthinking his wicketkeeping. He often reminds himself to trust that he'll react rather than trying to second-guess what may or may not happen. The more you hear him speak, the more you realise that this is a wicketkeeper who finds his rhythm from his mindset rather than from any technical triggers. He has clearly worked incredibly hard on his wicketkeeping, but the control of his mind has really driven his excellent performances of late. Some might say that this is because he's not enthralled by every microscopic element of wicketkeeping, but I think it would be a misjudgement. Time and time again, Jos would talk about something he had seen in another wicketkeeper that had helped him improve. This was evident when he told me about how he had noticed that famous arm swing that James Foster would do at the start of each day and often throughout a day of wicketkeeping.

> I would see him swinging his arms as if he was trying to make them long. I asked him about it, and he explained that it was to try to get all the tension out of his arms. I massively related to that because when I get nervous or negative while keeping, my arms get tense. I now consciously think about having dead or heavy hands because it relaxes my arms and then I keep at my best.

Towards the end of my time with Jos, I asked him if he had ever had any ridiculous advice from a teammate about wicketkeeping. The reason I asked this is because I think everyone has an opinion on wicketkeeping. It might be an unfounded one, but everyone will tell you what they think of a keeper. If you are perceived to be a 'keepers' keeper' then you are rarely, if ever, questioned. Those teammates will stand back as they subconsciously realise that they are out of their depth challenging this sort of keeper. But with someone deemed a 'batsman who is keeping', the floodgates can open! When I asked Jos about this, he told me a brilliant story:

> Yeah, I remember Ravi Bopara. I was starting to keep for England and was still very raw. I remember missing a few chances. In fact, I'd missed a stumping off Ravi the game before and the next game we were at Durham and I was catching off the bowlers while they loosened up before the game. And Ravi actually stood next to me while I did this and started saying things like, 'Look, you're not even watching the ball properly – what are you doing mate? You're not watching the ball mate.' He was stood a yard away from me and this was before a One Day International. I remember thinking, 'Look, I'm sorry I missed that stumping off you and I'm not a great keeper right now, but this is not helping me!' I laugh about it now but, looking back, it was a bit bizarre.

This hilarious little story sums up the life of a wicketkeeper. Ravi Bopara, who has never kept wicket seriously, could be sat in a commentary box one day telling the world that the keeper is just 'not watching the ball properly' and everyone would believe him!

I am glad that I spoke to Jos for this book. For someone who has achieved and continues to achieve as much as he does in the game, his humility is a lesson to so many others. He also revealed a lot about how the perception of someone like himself as a wicketkeeper can be a huge misjudgement. He was quick to acknowledge that he isn't as passionate about the art of wicketkeeping as others and sees it as another string to his bow, but the level of detail and thought he expressed in our hour together about wicketkeeping spoke volumes.

I came away from our chat feeling that Jos is actually very much what some would perceive as a real 'keeper'.

JOS BUTTLER CAREER AVERAGES

| Batting & Fielding | | | | | | | | | | |
Format	Matches	Innings	Runs	HS	Ave	SR	100s	50s	Ct	St
Test	56	98	2896	152	32.53	54.44	2	18	150	1
ODI	148	123	3872	150	38.72	118.66	9	20	181	32
T20I	88	80	2140	101*	34.51	141.16	1	15	39	10
FC	121	197	5877	152	32.46	57.35	7	33	271	3
List A	219	183	6038	150	43.12	119.46	11	36	233	37
T20	298	276	7335	124	32.45	144.02	2	50	163	34

†Statistics as of 15/01/2022

Chapter 4

Geraint Jones

'How close were you to playing for England?' is a question that my kids have asked me, as sometimes do people that I meet who want to ask me about my professional cricket career.

The short answer to that question is, 'Not very.'

However, I have to admit that I have pondered it once in a while. My honest answer is that I don't think I was ever that close to England selection but the year when I might have had the biggest chance was 2003.

In 2003, the England cricket team were going through some important changes under their head coach, Duncan Fletcher, which would eventually lead to that infamous 2005 Ashes series win. Chris Read took over as England's number 1 wicketkeeper at the end of that summer following the retirement of Alec Stewart. The winter tours prior to Christmas were to Bangladesh and Sri Lanka and unfortunately Read didn't seem to impress Fletcher, particularly with the bat.

The year 2003 also happened to be the one in which two other wicketkeepers in the country made their breakthrough in first-class cricket. They were ... me and Geraint Jones.

I was playing for Derbyshire in the second division of the County Championship and Geraint was playing for Kent in the first division. At the end of the season, I had scored 936 runs in the County Championship at an average of 37.44 and Geraint had scored 886 runs at an average of 44.30. My wicketkeeping was decent but certainly needed improving if I wanted to succeed on the international level. I think the same could have been said about Geraint's wicketkeeping at the time.

Geraint was selected as the back-up wicketkeeper to Chris Read on the tours of Bangladesh and Sri Lanka in 2003, and then the West Indies tour in 2004. In fact, on 10 April 2004, Geraint replaced Read in the England team for the 4th Test versus the West Indies in Antigua, in which Brian Lara scored 400 in one innings.

So, in my wishful thinking, I could ponder that 2003/4 was probably the closest I got to the England team, at least statistically. The reality is that Geraint was a much more dynamic cricketer than me and definitely suited where Duncan Fletcher wanted to take that England cricket team. I can still but dream!

When I prepared for my chat with Geraint Jones and read up on his statistics, I was surprised that he had only played thirty-four Test matches. In my head, I thought he had played a lot more, which is strange because he was a keeper of my era whom I closely watched and I would expect to know that sort of statistic. I realised that the reason I believed he had played more for England was because he had been involved in some huge Test matches that will long hang in my memory. Those powerful memories created an impression in my mind that Geraint had played much more.

His catch down the leg side of Michael Kasprowicz off the bowling of Steve Harmison at Edgbaston in 2005 to win an absolutely crucial Test match for England in that Ashes series is clearly the most powerful memory, but there are others. I will always remember Geraint's brilliant stumping of Andrew Hall from the last ball of the match off the bowling of Kabir Ali to win a One Day International against South Africa in Bloemfontein. South Africa needed one to win and Kabir was spearing yorkers in at around 85mph with some reverse swing. Geraint chose to stand up to the wicket to prevent the batsmen from running a single to him if the ball came through to him while he stood back. He knew that Kabir was going to attempt to bowl a yorker, which would be a very difficult ball for him to take cleanly. He would need to stay low, be calm and at his absolute best to catch the ball cleanly if it came to him. Kabir delivered the perfect yorker just wide of the off stump and Hall missed it. Geraint stayed down brilliantly and caught the ball perfectly to then stump Hall, who started to run, having missed the ball. It was a moment of wicketkeeping genius to win that One Day International.

I also have a less dramatic or glamourous memory of Geraint's wicketkeeping. It was when he was picked for his debut Test match in Antigua to replace Chris Read. England bowled first and Lara proceeded to plunder his way to 400. It meant that England were in the field for 202 overs. I was intrigued to see how Geraint would get on in his first Test and being in the field for over 200 overs was a tough start to his international wicketkeeping career. The wicket was very true, and it is fair to say that Lara wasn't leaving many balls alone outside the off stump, but that amount of time in the field really examines a wicketkeeper's fitness, concentration and technique. Chuck in some debut nerves and it requires a big effort. Geraint kept immaculately during that innings and it was only towards the very end of it that he let through four byes standing up to the bowling of Marcus Trescothick. Trescothick fired a ball down the leg side, which didn't give Geraint much chance and unfortunately the umpire didn't help him out by signalling four byes instead of wides, which is the great curse of wicketkeepers! With the West Indies' total of over 500 runs and Geraint yet to concede any byes, it would have been a world record if it had stayed that way. It was actually Trescothick's final ball of eighteen overs that he bowled. Bar that minor mistake, if you can call it that, Geraint was excellent behind the stumps in that match. I remember being really impressed.

I have to admit now that I absolutely loved my chat with Geraint for this chapter. He was a guy who achieved more than me with his career, but during our conversation I identified a lot with how he went about his cricket, particularly on the mental side of things. I also discovered a lot about him that I just didn't know previously. He is an impressive man.

The first thing to remember with Geraint is that he was effectively an Australian-styled wicketkeeper who landed in England at the age of 22. Prior to him, most of the England wicketkeepers followed a similar mould that was very much based on a Jack Russell type of technique, in which you would generally stand stiller standing back. Our Australian counterparts used their feet while standing back much more and Geraint was certainly from that school of technique. He talked of the role models he had while growing up in Queensland:

> Ian Healy and Wade Secombe were the main guys at Queensland at the time. Healy was the guy that I would watch the most and based my technique on, as a lot of Australian wicketkeepers did at that time. There's no doubt that Healy was my hero growing up. I remember reading Healy's book and he talked about keeping a diary

of his performances and trying to be immaculate with everything he did. It was in the old days where they would put whitener on their boots. I definitely fell in line with how he brought such organisation and work to his game, it really resonated with me. You see, I could move naturally but catching certainly wasn't my most natural ability. So, being organised and working hard stayed with me my whole career and helped me a lot. It actually gave me a calming effect as I could hook onto those things for how I went about things.

Geraint's comment that catching wasn't his most natural ability was fascinating. A fan hearing this of an England wicketkeeper might be completely shocked, especially one who perceives that wicketkeepers live and breathe to catch any object they can. I have already talked about how people's perceptions of wicketkeepers tend to differ wildly, and this can shape conversations and assessments of them. I think people often loosely say of wicketkeepers, 'He or she's got good hands,' yet here was an England wicketkeeper openly admitting that his hands were what needed most work within his skills.

Geraint even extended this beyond his wicketkeeping, saying: 'I never saw myself as a natural. I always had natural talent as a sports player, playing all sorts of different sports. But as a cricketer, I never had a natural sort of feeling about that.'

It was incredible honesty from Geraint, which gave me an amazing insight into who he was as a person and how he had been successful at the highest levels of cricket. I suddenly realised that I didn't know that much about him as a person, in spite of having been around him for many years of my career.

I learned resilience to deal with and overcome challenges. I lost my mum when I was 11 years old, and, you know, it was a massive, massive blow to me. Probably one that affected me far more than I ever realised, even to this day. Sport was how I got over it. So, that resilience was linked with that loss. Without me even realising, that resilience I learned as a young lad who lost his mum at 11 helped me deal with stuff in my cricket career and carry on.

It is very true in life that we rarely know what is going on in somebody else's head. The loss that Geraint suffered as a young boy had absolutely shaped who he was and driven him to become an international wicketkeeper, despite not being a natural catcher. That alone should blow up anyone's perception that wicketkeepers are all the same. Geraint was determined to succeed as a wicketkeeper regardless of what stood in his way. His mindset was fascinating, inspiring, and different to several of the other wicketkeepers I spoke to. Some felt that they were creating art while wicketkeeping; for Geraint, it was different. It was a challenge that he was determined to overcome and succeed in. It just happened to be that cricket and, within that, wicketkeeping was his focus.

I always had an internal battle with my wicketkeeping because I knew I made mistakes, and I made some absolute dog easy mistakes. And so, I always felt that there was another group of keepers who were on a completely different level to me; and that's where I was trying to get through to. My time spent working hard

was to try to get to a position where it looked natural.
I always fought myself massively on the perception of
my keeping.

This was something I identified with very much. At times
during my career, I also fought with my own perception of my
wicketkeeping – I was too tall, I didn't move well enough, my
stance wasn't quite right and so on. Of course, there is some
normal insecurity within this that most people have in areas
of their lives, but I come back to the point that many people
see wicketkeeping as some sort of art form. There is a style and
a grace to it. When we watch a violinist performing exquisitely,
we don't wonder whether the musician is fighting an internal
battle while they perform. We simply sit back and enjoy the
beauty of the music.

As you know, one of the reasons I wanted to write this book
was to break down many of the preconceived perceptions
people have about wicketkeepers and illustrate how broad and
wonderful a community it is. What I hadn't realised to this
point in my conversation with Geraint was that wicketkeepers
themselves might suffer under their own preconceived ideas as
to what a wicketkeeper should look and sound like, including me!

Following this, I moved the conversation to how it felt for
Geraint when he was keeping well.

There were no personal battles going on, it just flowed –
there was rhythm. I'm a big one on feel. You can feel in
the rhythm of wicketkeeping, even in training. I loved the
repetition of training and getting that feel of rhythm with

whoever you're working with. And on the back of that, I avoided wicketkeeping drills which took away from my rhythm. I remember watching Matt Prior working with Bruce French and he had the bowling machine close and he was in the full padded gear. They were working at high speed off the ramps and it was all reactionary stuff. I looked into it, but I avoided it because to get trust in myself, I wanted that feeling of rhythm and repetition all the time. If I then threw myself into sessions that took it away, I didn't feel comfortable. So, when I was keeping out in the middle, that's what I searched for. I didn't want that jerkiness. I wanted smoothness. At my best, I would slow things down. Slowing it down was to take away the anxiety of what was coming and to focus on what I was doing, which allowed me just to react. I always wanted to feel right at the moment of ball release, whether batting or keeping, that I wanted to be in the best position I could be.

Flow and rhythm were words also used by Jos Buttler and I suspect will keep coming up in this book. It reminds me of how I described watching Jack Russell keep wicket for the first time. Wicketkeepers are categorised as the 'drummers in the band' because of their lynchpin status in a team but perhaps they are actually working off their own drumbeat ... a gentle beat in their minds that is controlling their movements, and when that is perfectly in sync then there is a grace and ease to it, even a beauty.

All wicketkeepers, particularly England ones, have been the focus of sharp criticism during their careers. I remember Geraint being at the brunt end of this when he dropped Shane Warne in the 2005 Ashes at Old Trafford. Duncan Fletcher, the England head coach at the time, defended Geraint, pointing out that other leading wicketkeepers around the world also made mistakes.

'I've seen Gilchrist drop his, I've seen Mark Boucher drop many, I've seen Kumar Sangakkara drop many,' Fletcher said.

With this in mind and hearing Geraint talk so openly about his internal battles with his wicketkeeping, it prompted me to ask the question: 'Now that you look back on your career, did you spend most of your time as a keeper thinking, "Don't make a mistake!" or "I'm going to take a brilliant catch in a minute"?'

Another reason for asking this question is that I know I spent most of my career thinking the former. The biggest one-day game I played was the 2006 C&G final at Lord's versus Sussex. I had an excellent game with the gloves, with three catches and a stumping, but throughout the whole time in the field, all I was thinking was, 'Don't make a f*cking mistake!' It was actually an exhausting mindset to have and one that Geraint and I shared.

Yeah, I guess I was the more negative mindset because I was aware of my mistakes. I had a coach when I was first in the Kent Second XI who used to say to me, 'I bet you a pound you drop a ball this session,' and I would just say, 'Yeah, I will drop one,' because I was always fighting against the mistakes that would happen. Where I flipped it around was in the moment of a mistake, I recovered from it quickly. I didn't dwell on it in the moment. They would keep me awake for hours at night-time. In fact, outside of the game, it really dogged me. But in the game, I was determined to make amends and show my teammates what I was about. I would say in my head, 'I've made that mistake, but this is the real me. This is what I can do.'

In essence, Geraint was talking about accepting that he would make mistakes and moving on from them quickly. Jos Buttler talked of something similar. It is clear that Geraint spent a large part of his career dealing with the mental side of his wicketkeeping. He had his own internal battles with how he perceived his wicketkeeping and was also aware of how he was perceived from the outside. As I mentioned earlier, I think for wicketkeepers that some people don't see as a 'keepers' keeper', they can get bombarded with people giving their opinion on what they are doing wrong or what they should do that they are not already doing. It is another strange dynamic that doesn't exist in any other area of cricket. Someone who has never seriously kept wicket can feel the authority to tell you what is right for your wicketkeeping, while we would never imagine a number 11 batsman wandering up to the opening batsman and telling them what is right for them. I asked every wicketkeeper in this book about this to see what was the strangest advice or thing that has happened to them on this front. This was Geraint's recollection:

> I remember something with Rob Key when he got frustrated with me. I remember a clash at Tunbridge Wells where I'd just been dropped by England from the Pakistan series. I had actually broken my finger, but I was going to get dropped anyway. It was the first time in my career that I had my hands X-rayed and I had chipped the top of my right-hand ring finger. I was wringing my hand a lot while wicketkeeping because of the pain and Keysey

seemed to get frustrated with that. He was fielding at cover, and ball after ball, he would just hurl the ball back at me as hard as he could, basically to say, 'Get on with it.'

There is literally no other area of cricket in which this could happen. Your wicketkeeper is playing with a broken finger so you throw the ball at him as hard as you can because you're frustrated about how he is dealing with his broken finger! It would be like us telling a batsman to run faster knowing that they had torn their hamstring or telling a bowler to bowl faster when we know they have a side strain. Talk about the game not slowing down for wicketkeepers! It's another brilliant little story that highlights the life of a wicketkeeper.

As I have said, I didn't really know Geraint personally during my career but after my chat with him, I felt like I knew him well, and I liked him a lot. There is no question that he maxed out his career. He got from it everything that his talent and hard work could possibly muster, and the loss of his mother had a huge impact on nurturing this determination and resilience. In cricket, and in life, we are well to be reminded that we often know little of what is going inside someone else's head despite how strong or secure they may look. Losing your mother at 11 years old would clearly have a major impact on anyone but to understand how Geraint survived and thrived as an international wicketkeeper, you need to appreciate this particular point.

Geraint might never have felt like some other keepers on the circuit and continuously dealt with internal battles, but he threw his heart and soul into the role. He played eighty-seven times for England as a wicketkeeper and deserved every single one of those caps.

GERAINT JONES CAREER AVERAGES

Batting & Fielding									
Format	Matches	Innings	Runs	HS	Ave	SR	100s	50s	Ct	St
Test	34	53	1172	100	23.91	54.13	1	6	128	5
ODI	51	43	862	80	24.62	77.17	0	4	68	4
T20I	2	2	33	19	33	132	0	0	2	0
FC	203	309	9087	178	32.45	–	15	50	599	36
List A	213	176	3679	87	25.72	82.04	0	17	209	42
T20	127	100	1529	56	18.87	114.7	0	3	55	26

Chapter 5

Chris Read

Duncan Fletcher once asked me if it was possible when
I saw someone going down for the sweep that I could hit
the deck and get my pads in the way, a bit like a hockey
goalkeeper. I was, like, well my job is to catch the ball …

There's no question in my eyes that Chris Read was one of the
two purest wicketkeepers of my era (James Foster being the
other). Put simply, Chris was exceptional. The above quote
from him from our chat together said so much to me about how
he viewed wicketkeeping. Yes, being a keeper was his job, but
it was also so much more to him than that. It was a passion, a
search for perfection … dare I say it, an obsession. His love of
wicketkeeping came from the richest traditions of the role. He
saw that his job was to catch every single ball of every single
day of cricket that he played in – simply, in his mind, that is
what a wicketkeeper did. And that is why Fletcher's suggestion
was so strange to him. It went against the purity of what a
wicketkeeper did.

'For me, wicketkeeping is an art form and one in which
I wanted to be, a bit like my personality, as efficient and functional
as possible.'

There are a few different ways to look back on Chris Read's
international career but two things are clear to me:

1. At 20 years old, he was picked at a very young age and a few years away from his peak with both gloves and bat. As a comparison, at the same age I was scrambling around in Somerset's second team.

2. His career sat bang in the middle of a time when Adam Gilchrist was having a huge impact on world cricket, which meant the role of the wicketkeeper was being reconsidered in English cricket. This was being strongly driven by the then head coach, Duncan Fletcher.

The odd part of writing this is that it sounds like Chris was a below average batsman. This clearly wasn't the case with a first-class average of 37.26 versus Geraint Jones's 32.45. Granted, his batting improved throughout his career, but that is normal. I would also add that Fletcher was definitely looking for a counter-attacking batsman as his England wicketkeeper during this time. Geraint Jones fitted the bill, but I would strongly argue that Chris Read did as well. Being in the opposition to many painful partnerships with Chris and the Nottinghamshire middle order is testament to that!

As I have already explained, I think keepers pick up their identity as a true wicketkeeper in their teens. Those cricketers that people perceive as a 'keepers' keeper' have had that persona well before they play professional cricket. This was true of Chris, but he also identified as an all-rounder.

Bar a little wobble in my late teens, I really was a 'keeper' once I started with it. But, rightly or wrongly, I always wanted to keep wicket and open the batting. It was because I had started as a batsman from Under-11s.

I never wanted to be a keeper and bat 7. I always felt there were two very distinct strings to my bow. But at the same time, yeah, keeping was definitely my thing.

I truly believe that timing played a massive role in Chris's England career. In my opinion, Fletcher saw Chris as a 'keepers' keeper' who was brilliant with the gloves but not strong enough with the bat, and instead saw Geraint Jones as his perfect mould for England's version of Adam Gilchrist – not as good with the gloves but a match-changing batsman. I think this in itself is a misunderstanding of how good Gilchrist was as a wicketkeeper. I just think Chris needed more time to develop as an all-rounder at that level. He definitely didn't just see himself as an out-and-out keeper and his batting roots from his junior years were still very much in place as he made his way through professional cricket.

Of all the elite wicketkeepers I have watched throughout my life, Chris Read made the biggest technical changes during a professional career. In truth, this is extremely rare. Of course, keepers tinker with technique all the time but to make such a shift is very unusual, especially from someone who had already played for England.

By the time I was 22 years old, I had already played for and been dropped by England. I almost felt like I was coming back down the other side of it. I remember having, by my standards, a poor year behind stumps. Whether it was a whole season or just a patch in the season, I can't remember, but it wasn't the standard I expected of myself. That winter was my first winter when I wasn't picked for anything; I was out of sight, basically. So I thought, 'OK, first let's make the most of this.' I remember looking at Gilchrist and noticing that he was similar to Healy in terms of method, and also extremely consistent. I started to wonder whether this was something to look at. He was standing back to McGrath and standing up to Warne, and very rarely made a mistake. I was working with Bruce French at the time and I remember talking to him at the beginning of our first session in November or December that winter. I wanted to explore this Australian method a little bit. Why do they use their feet so much? Why do they catch it on the inside? Why do they catch it with such a long length of catch? Frenchy and I basically went on a journey with it together. It just wasn't something that was talked about in English cricket at the time. And I quickly found that the rhythmical nature of that method of continually moving or looking to move really suited me. I would dive less and feel less rushed when there was a nick, instead of reacting from a static position. And I quickly really warmed to it and loved it and embraced it.

The good thing was I had whole winter of five months to craft it and see if there were any pros and cons before testing it out in the middle. That became my method and, in truth, it was a 'Hallelujah' moment with my keeping, and at a very early age. From then on, it was just a case of fine-tuning that throughout my career. I think over time it probably became a bit of a hybrid between what we've determined old English model and a more Australian model.

I played against Chris many times throughout my career and the comfort in which he held his wicketkeeping technique was obvious to see. He never looked in doubt with his glovework. I have already spoken about the inner battles that both myself and Geraint Jones had with our keeping, but Chris was so in tune with his technique that he never faced this.

> I don't recall feeling any doubt. Once my technique was established or very well established, I always trusted and had faith in it; and it very rarely let me down to the point I felt awful or clunky.

This might sound simple enough and a mindset or headspace that most elite wicketkeepers eventually reach, but not all do. I would never put myself in Chris Read's bracket, but I was still a first-class wicketkeeper for many years, and I didn't reach that point of comfort that Chris describes. Many wicketkeepers battle with a technical, physical or mental deficiency throughout their career. They can hide it extremely well, but it lingers in the back of their mind and nags at them when they make a mistake. It really is only the purest of wicketkeepers who manages to find that almost perfect rhythm and flow to their wicketkeeping for long periods of time.

> At my best, it felt like a flow that was rhythmical from set-up to catch – there was no jerkiness, no pause, it was just 'set and move', chuck the ball away and repeat. If I was in a period where I was fine-tuning or not catching it as well, then it would just feel like everything wasn't in sync. And the whole rhythm thing was about repetition,

just being able to repeat the same thing over and over again. And that's why my keeping method really worked for me – it was essentially me catching the same way every single ball.

The more I spoke with Chris, the more I realised that the precision to which he kept wicket was perfectly aligned with the precision in which he studied it. He is a library of wicketkeeping knowledge clearly mixed with what was an incredible determination to be the best.

I had that inner drive to be one of the best keepers around and that probably stemmed from early on in my career. Around the time I made my England debut there was obviously Healy and Russell on the international stage, but domestically there were guys like Piper, Rhodes, Hegg and Metson. They were all exceptional keepers. It seemed like every county had a top keeper. Like I've said, throughout my early career my batting was on an equal footing to my keeping. I didn't see myself as a keeper who batted or a batter who kept wicket. I just wanted to bat as well as I could when I did and be the best keeper I could be when I kept; but I definitely wanted to be regarded in the same league as the top tier of the keepers that I have mentioned – that was my ambition.

Chris was someone so in tune with who he was as a wicketkeeper that he really did embody all that it involved. It very much reminded me of talking to Sarah Taylor. And it might just be this exact thing that makes people refer to someone like Chris or Sarah as a 'keepers' keeper'. It is not just the quality of their keeping but their embodiment of the art form – their engrossment in or obsession with it. It is more than just a job. For example, Adam Gilchrist was an incredibly consistent wicketkeeper and Alec Stewart reached outstanding levels with the gloves, but neither would be referred to as a 'keepers' keeper'. I think the great misunderstanding by many watching and commentating on cricket is that they don't truly believe that a keeper can be elite without being what they perceive to be the personification of a true wicketkeeper. I just don't think this is true. Gilchrist was exceptional but arguably far less of an embodiment of a traditional keeper than Jack Russell, but ultimately it mattered little.

No wicketkeeper is perfect throughout their career and, of course, Chris was no different. His mistakes were rare but, like all keepers, he never forgot them.

> Every catch or stumping that I knew I should have taken but didn't is heavily imprinted on my mind. There are two particular mistakes that I will never forget. We were toiling at Edgbaston because we always seemed to play on very good pitches. I think Warwickshire always thought we were gung-ho and flaky in our approach so they thought if we just bat and bat, we would come out swinging and get ourselves out – which was pretty much correct, to be fair! We had gone toe to toe to them in the game and Samit Patel bowled one to Chris Wright, who was in at number 10 or 11 for Warwickshire. Chris came down the wicket, it went through the gate and missed leg stump – so, definitely a tricky one but I saw it all the way and didn't react quick enough and missed the stumping.

He then went on to get 70-odd, and from level pegging, they then went on to get a hundred lead and won the game. I remember feeling sick about it. I knew that probably our chance of winning or drawing that game went when I missed that stumping, and that was horrible. But probably the worst one was when I dropped Ben Stokes on a horrible day up in Durham for a quarter- or semi-final in one of the One Day International cups. It was nibbling all over the place and we had them in big trouble. Steve Mullaney nipped one away and got the edge of Stokes's bat. I was standing up and it went straight in and straight out my gloves. Stokes went on to score 160, which would have been a decent team score on that wicket and, of course, we lost.

As Chris described these mistakes, I knew, as a former keeper, that they were both fairly tough chances. It made me smile inwardly because I missed MUCH easier chances than that! It said volumes for the difference in quality of keeper between Chris and me.

When I began writing this book, I did feel the perception of the pure wicketkeeper was overplayed by certain commentators in the game nowadays. I felt it came from nostalgic memories of Bob Taylor and Alan Knott, and actually plays down how good many of the keepers are in today's game that are not perceived as out-and-out wicketkeepers. Overall, I still hold this opinion because I believe that the performance of a wicketkeeper is often viewed through subjective eyes and dependent on how someone perceives they should look and sound like. As a small example,

Chris himself fell foul to this when Duncan Fletcher's opinion was that wicketkeepers should be louder and more aggressive than Chris naturally was. However, I must admit that as I chatted to Chris and absorbed everything he said, I felt that there was something more to what he was about than others. His hunger for perfection within the art form of wicketkeeping reminded me of how Jimmy Anderson approaches seam bowling. They are master craftsmen of their skills, and with that a certain grace comes to their performance.

As the cricket journalist Tim Wigmore wrote: 'Wicketkeeping in the modern age has become largely a functional pursuit; to see Read was to be reminded of what it can still be elevated to: artistry.'

I am glad that Chris has moved into coaching, just as I am with Sarah Taylor. They hold the role of wicketkeeper on a different level to many others and, for them, even coaching it will be more than just about earning money. They will pass on that deep passion for the role to the next generation. They care deeply about how to produce high-quality wicketkeeping, and this was really summed up for me here:

> I captained for basically 50 per cent of my career and I remember in my second year of captaining the T20, I ended up speaking to Mick Newell to tell him I was actually shot with it. My keeping standards had dropped during the intensity of T20. While the bowler was running up to bowl, I was thinking about who needed to bowl next! Between Mick and I, we decided that I would stand down as T20 captain to get my standards back to where they should have been with the gloves.

Almost the exact same thing had happened to me while I was captain of Derbyshire. I really struggled to keep up with the T20 game while captaining and keeping, and my keeping suffered for it. However, the big difference is that despite me recognising this, I didn't give up the captaincy. The captaincy was so important to me that I would ignore the fact that my keeping wasn't where it should have been. The opposite can be said for Chris, and this says so much about how he viewed the importance of glovework – it came above all else, including captaincy.

So, on a final point, could a wicketkeeper as pure and brilliant as Chris Read look on at any other keeper in the world and feel an ounce of jealousy?

> Yeah, for sure! The major assets to my keeping were definitely my footwork stood back and to spin on a day 4 wicket. That was really fun for me and I felt like I would rise to the occasion if I was keeping to Swann or McGill on a spinning wicket. I actually remember those days the fondest. But when I looked around my peers, the one area that I never reached the heights of Russell or Foster was standing up to the seamers. I actually think the nature of our Nottinghamshire attack and our wickets meant I didn't get as much opportunity to do it as those guys. But when those guys were in their absolute zone, it was amazing. I remember watching Fozzy keeping to Graham Napier, stood up, while he bowled 85 miles per hour on a skiddy one at Chelmsford and just make it look so simple. I remember thinking, 'Gee, that is seriously impressive, and I wish I could do that.'

That might just say as much about the quality of James Foster as anything else.

I have no doubt that in another era and certainly under a different England head coach, Chris Read could have played more than fifty Test matches for England. He was an exceptional all-round cricketer and a true gloveman, and if we are to label someone a 'keepers' keeper', then Chris is definitely one of them.

He was a true master of the craft of wicketkeeping.

CHRIS READ CAREER AVERAGES

| Batting & Fielding | | | | | | | | | | |
Format	Matches	Innings	Runs	HS	Ave	SR	100s	50s	Ct	St
Test	15	23	360	55	18.94	39.47	0	1	48	6
ODI	36	24	300	30*	17.64	73.17	0	0	41	2
T20I	1	1	13	13	13	118.18	0	0	1	0
FC	349	526	16361	240	37.26	–	26	92	1051	53
List A	333	265	5564	135	29.13	–	2	24	319	73
T20	119	98	1441	58*	23.24	124.22	0	1	60	27

Chapter 6

Sarah Taylor

There have been many moments in the last ten years in which women's cricket has stood up to be noticed … moments when the cynics and doubters of the women's game have had to take a day off (thankfully).

Sarah Taylor's wicketkeeping has been responsible for more than a few of those moments. Her one-handed catch of the Australian captain Jodie Fields, as she reverse-swept Danielle Hazell in 2013, was breathtaking, and her leg-side stumping of Ellyse Perry off the bowling of Natalie Sciver in 2019 was Jack Russell/Gladstone Small/Dean Jones-esk. But the piece of skill that blew my mind was when she stumped the South African Suné Luus first ball off the bowling of Anya Shrubsole in 2018. It was a full ball, speared down the leg side, which then bounced more than normal. Sarah's movement down the leg side was fast and slick and she reacted to the extra bounce by catching the ball one-handed in her left hand before stumping Luus. It was phenomenal.

In a thirteen-year international career with 226 caps, Sarah Taylor will always be remembered as one of the finest wicketkeepers this country has ever produced, and that is in both men's and women's cricket. In fact, her quality triggered Adam Gilchrist to comment in 2018 that she was the best wicketkeeper in the world. That is some compliment from a true legend of the game.

On a personal level, I have watched Sarah keep wicket for many years and was immediately struck by the smoothness of her keeping. There was always a flow to it as if the movements she made were without force and in perfect timing. It was impossible to watch her and not know that you were watching a high-quality wicketkeeper. I have also read many of the articles about her battles with mental health. I have admired her from a distance on both fronts and, as a result, she was very high on my list of keepers to interview for this book. I had never met her before our chat and was intrigued to see where it would go. She was one of the few keepers that I really knew little about other than what I had read in the media.

So, where did it all start?

> I was playing for Sussex Under-15s when I was about 11 years old and for one match the wicketkeeper didn't turn up. At that point I was just a fairly loud and annoying fielder who always wanted to be involved. The coach at the time asked me to try keeping for that reason really. I'll never forget it.

As soon as Sarah started talking about wicketkeeping, I knew that there was something deep with it for her. This was definitely not just a job in cricket.

> I'll never forget the ball hitting my gloves for the first time, I just loved it. I was involved in the game, all the time. I felt in control – in control of my environment. I just fell in love with it.

From the first time that Sarah tried wicketkeeping for Sussex Under-15s there was no looking back. This would be her passion, her obsession – it would be 'her'.

> I love Test cricket, I'll watch it all night; but as everyone else is watching the bowling or the batting, I'm watching the keeper – where they are stood, how they catch the ball, just everything they are doing. That's how I view cricket. That was and still is me.

As Sarah said all these things, there was a real intensity about her love of wicketkeeping. She readily admits that she is naturally talented behind the stumps, but I believe that it is her love for it that drives everything. She heavily credits the influence of her first coach, Nick Wilton, and then, more latterly, Michael Bates, for drilling the basics of wicketkeeping into her and allowing her to be a sponge to all the information that they could pass on.

'It really annoys me when I hear the phrase "someone has been moulded into a keeper". You can't be moulded into a true wicketkeeper – you are born a keeper.'

If ever there was a phrase to sum up Sarah's passion for wicketkeeping, there it was – 'you are born to be a keeper'. It was a fascinating insight. It was similar to my conversation with Chris Read but maybe even on another level. Of course, wicketkeeping is about skills and technique for Sarah, but there was more to it than this. I'm trying not to be overdramatic, but it felt like wicketkeeping was the place that Sarah felt like she truly belonged in life.

As someone who has experienced similar problems, I have always been drawn to the media interviews and articles about Sarah's issues with her mental health. Her honesty and bravery in speaking up and explaining it to the world have been amazing and will have helped countless others find the courage to talk about the struggles they are having. As Sarah and I talked, I couldn't help but wonder if her deep passion or even obsession with wicketkeeping had a part in her mental health challenges. Wicketkeepers are the only breed in cricket who try to be perfect every single day. The levels of expectation they place on themselves and that others place on them are like nothing a bowler or a batsman will experience. A keeper of Sarah's quality will expect to go through a whole day's play and literally catch every ball perfectly. Not even Jimmy Anderson would expect himself to bowl every single ball perfectly during a day's play. Did the intense desire to be perfect play a role in her declining mental health? Was it a heavy burden to carry for someone so driven to be the best at wicketkeeping?

'No, it didn't, actually. I just love wicketkeeping. It was more the batting that played on my mind. I love keeping so much; it's really natural to me.'

Sarah talked more of the burden of batting in an interview with the *Daily Telegraph* in 2019 in which she remembers a tour of the Caribbean in 2013:

> I wanted to go home but I didn't really understand why or what the excuse was in my head. I couldn't justify it. At one point I said to one of the coaches, 'I'm not feeling great; I'd quite like to go home.' He said exactly what I'd probably have said: 'Don't worry, things will pick up, the

runs will come, and you'll feel fine.' At the time I was like, 'Yeah he's right.'

And then, in an Ashes game in Melbourne a few months later, Sarah was due to come out in her normal position at number 3.

'I ended up having to run off and be sick. I didn't know why. I ended up panicking so much that I vomited.'

And two years later, after the T20 World Cup in India, Sarah said, 'I didn't want to go bat, I didn't want to play cricket, I didn't want to do anything.'

Even how Sarah learned to deal with mistakes is a reflection of the calmness she found within wicketkeeping.

It has changed over my career. When I was young, I was quite naïve and was just like, 'Oh well', and didn't really think about it. As I got more settled in the England team, I obviously knew that mistakes would cost the team more and if I dropped one then I would feel like I had let the team down. But then I just learned to make it a process thing. I took the emotion out of it. If I dropped a catch, I would look at why and then go and correct it. That was it. It became more process than emotion, so I would move on very quickly. My teammates always knew that I was trying to be perfect so if I made a mistake, they knew I would work to correct it.

Dare I say it, but maybe wicketkeeping is just a happy place for Sarah. It reminded me of when she described the first time that she kept wicket. She said that she felt 'in control of her environment'. In a world of so many unpredictable outcomes and the high pressure of elite sport, anxiety can play a huge role in someone's mind; but wicketkeeping wasn't this place for Sarah. It was *her* space. This is something much deeper and more powerful than it ever being just a job or a role in a cricket team.

Sarah used the word 'natural' to describe her keeping so many times and there was definitely something in that. Like, for instance, when I asked her how it felt when she was keeping well:

> Nothing. Can I say that? It is just like, I am doing. I don't think; I just do. I don't like complication or overthinking and when I am keeping it is just easy and natural, I am just doing. It's batting that makes me overthink.

When I asked Jos Buttler what he would do if he went to practice and could only bat or keep wicket, he said that he would definitely bat and back himself to be natural in the game with the gloves. He actually felt that that was a reflection of the fact that he didn't see himself as a 'keepers' keeper'; but Sarah actually said exactly the same: 'Keeping is so natural to me that I didn't want to overcomplicate it with too much technical stuff; so, at practice I would definitely bat and leave the keeping to my natural instincts in the match.'

In a cricketing world in which everyone has an opinion on what wicketkeepers should sound and look like, this was interesting. Jos Buttler has been labelled as not necessarily a true wicketkeeper and more of a batsman moulded into one, but in this case, he actually would have the same practice routine as a master craftsman of wicketkeeping like Sarah.

There's no question that Sarah has enormous confidence in her wicketkeeping and doesn't sit comparing herself with other keepers around the world, whether male or female. As a student of the art of wicketkeeping, there has been nothing that she has seen in world cricket that has made her question whether she could do that.

> No, I haven't ever felt that way. I'm very comfortable with what I can do. I enjoy watching what other wicketkeepers are doing, particularly in Test cricket, and pick things up. I made a conscious decision to get my gloves as close to the line of the stumps as possible when standing up because I saw Dhoni doing it. I could see it reduced the time to stump someone.

I was fortunate to manage Jimmy Anderson for nearly a decade and I saw how much he studied what other bowlers were doing around the world. I would go around to his house and he would always have cricket on the TV, whether red or white ball cricket, and he was watching the bowlers. Someone would bowl a certain type of slower ball and he would be immediately studying how they did. Sometimes young cricketers today feel embarrassed to say how much they love watching cricket; it's not 'cool'. But with both Jimmy and Sarah, masters of what they do, they share that obsession for information about their craft. There's no accident in the link between that and how brilliant they are at what they do.

As per every other wicketkeeper in this book, I asked Sarah if she was ever on the receiving end of some crazy keeping advice from anyone who has never kept wicket seriously in their lives before.

> Yeah, I have actually. I'm not going to name names, but one particular England bowler used to do it all the time.

In the end, I would just say, 'Listen, why don't you have a go with the gloves then?' That normally quietened things down!

This question brought us onto the subject of why everyone seems to have such a big opinion on wicketkeepers versus other positions in the team.

I think it's because of the high consequences of our job. If we make a mistake, then it could have really big consequences for the match. It's the same in football with goalkeepers. Because of this, everyone is always closely watching the keepers and quick to criticise.

I hadn't heard that before and I think it is a brilliant viewpoint on the question. As I am writing this, England have just lost to Italy in the final of the European Football Championships in a penalty shoot-out. Jordan Pickford, the England goalkeeper, was brilliant throughout the tournament, alongside a number of outfield players. Pickford also saved two Italian penalties in the shoot-out. The consequences of any mistakes he might have made throughout the tournament would have been huge, in just the same way as if a wicketkeeper dropped, for example, Steve Smith in an Ashes Test match. I think Sarah is absolutely right – the reason that everyone wants their say on a wicketkeeper, or goalkeeper, for that matter, is because it is a bloody important position! As people view that position as a fan or pundit, they want that person to be excellent at their job. Mistakes will always be big talking points.

This is the reason why some people found it so hard to stomach when Duncan Fletcher said he could handle the odd drop catch if his keeper scored more runs. It could be the equivalent of a football manager saying he didn't mind his keeper letting in the odd goal as long as he was good with his feet in passing from the back. When you say things like this about such a high-stakes position in the team then it is clearly going to stir debate. And the debate will polarise opinion between people who see the tradition and purity of the role and those who want to see the role move to something new.

The high consequences viewpoint that Sarah gave me also made me reflect on why wicketkeepers are so special. They live a sporting life on the finest of lines between hero and villain, and this is in a game in which the majority of people don't really have a clue what you're doing. It's an incredibly precarious position to be in. As James Foster once said: 'People almost see you as being there not to make a mistake, which is a poor psychological opinion on a wicketkeeper, but that is what it is and it's probably going to be around forever.'

I didn't know where this book would take me, but I was determined to let the wicketkeepers lead the narrative through their stories and experiences. More than anyone else I spoke to, Sarah Taylor showed me what being a 'keepers' keeper' is really like. Put to one side technique or mindset or obsession, or even quality, Sarah is a true wicketkeeper in my opinion because it is part of the very essence of who she is. It is where she feels the most natural. It is where she can express herself without having to overthink or overcomplicate things in her mind. It is where she feels the most control in life. Wicketkeeping makes her happy; in fact, it makes her *really* happy. Whether the fact that she became one of the world's best wicketkeepers is connected to this is something we won't ever really know, and I am not entirely sure that it matters much.

My chat with Sarah was an eye-opener in many ways – and I am a wicketkeeper; I come from the same world of cricket that she does. Her identity with being a wicketkeeper was way beyond what I or a number of other keepers I spoke to for this book felt. It kept bringing me back to how Jimmy Anderson approaches his seam bowling – there is a deep connection with the art of it. As Sarah now moves into coaching, I wondered if this ever frustrates her when she coaches a young keeper who doesn't feel the same about wicketkeeping as she does.

> Yeah, sometimes. I can coach a young keeper with a load of talent but no great passion for what's involved; and then someone with loads of passion but limited ability. It can be frustrating because ideally you want the talented one to truly understand how brilliant they could be as a keeper if they fully embraced it.

As a coach, Sarah is looking for that perfect combination of ability and a deep-rooted passion for the art of wicketkeeping in her young keepers, and ultimately, that is what the likes of Sarah and Jimmy Anderson are – a perfect combination of ability and passion.

That is what makes them so brilliant.

I came away from my time with Sarah understanding that there are different levels to being a wicketkeeper and she is on the very top tier. And to be on that tier, forget about being moulded into it; you might just have to be born that way.

SARAH TAYLOR CAREER AVERAGES

| Batting & Fielding | | | | | | | | | |
Format	Matches	Innings	Runs	HS	Ave	SR	100s	50s	Ct	St
WTEST	10	17	**300**	40	18.75	49.58	0	0	18	2
WODI	126	119	**4056**	147	38.26	82.32	7	20	87	51
WT20I	90	87	**2177**	77	29.02	110.67	0	16	23	51

†Statistics as of 15/01/2022

Chapter 7

Jack Russell

I don't think I could have written this book without speaking to Jack Russell.

He was the very reason I wanted to be a wicketkeeper and he was truly the benchmark for wicketkeepers of my era in style and quality. The vast majority of us just wanted to be like Jack. When he moved his stance to face the off side more when standing back to seamers, many of us, including me, did the same simply because that's what he did. We attempted to mimic the way his arms hung down relaxed by his side as if his gloves were heavy. We wanted our kit to look like his, whether it was the pads with a bigger groove on top of the shoe or the way his gloves just looked massive. More than anything, we wanted to catch the ball like Jack as if it was our most natural instinct in the world. Many cricketers had a huge influence on me but for pure wicketkeeping, Jack was unparalleled.

Jack also had an enormous impact on a generation of cricket fans over their perception of what a wicketkeeper should look like. His quirks, his mystery, the hat, the gloves … everything about him amplified the persona of what a true wicketkeeper should look like in their eyes. This was simply a reflection on how much Jack was admired and loved by fans. During my research for this book I spoke to a varied selection of international wicketkeepers, all of whom should be considered highly successful for the simple reason that they reached the top of the game. But some of these keepers have been very different to Jack in technique and style; some haven't been considered a 'keepers' keeper'; some have been labelled as 'more of a batsman'; and some have even been honest enough to say that they struggled with catching. My aim for this book was to show people what a wide tent the wicketkeeping community truly is and what makes them tick despite the differences. I wanted to show how exceptional I think wicketkeepers are. However, to do this I felt I needed the reference of the one wicketkeeper who has influenced the role more than any other of my era and the era before. So, without speaking to Jack, I just don't think this book would have been right. In the end, I had the most fascinating ninety minutes of conversation with him. The insight he gave me was engrossing and I actually found it difficult to condense it all into one chapter. I hold Jack in the highest esteem and our chat only enhanced that perception. He's the Wicketkeeping King for me.

In the second Test match I watched live, I observed Jack keep wicket. I know there were other cricketers performing but I was watching Jack. I was enthralled by him – a small man doing something with such rhythm and grace that made it look like an art form. He commanded my attention; in fact, he commanded the attention of everyone on the field. I wanted to do what Jack was doing. I embarrassed him by telling him about the impact that he had on me and he explained to me that the same has happened for him:

Well, there was a pivotal moment for me, a bit like for you. In 1977, England were playing the Aussies and Alan Knott caught Rick McCosker diving to his right-hand side one-handed in front of Mike Brearley at first slip.

The bowler was Tony Greig. He also caught Rodney Marsh down the leg side off Beefy. But it was actually the Rick McCosker catch that made me go, 'I want to do that for England.' That was the spark. That was the moment when I thought, 'Right, I'm going to do that.'

During a time when there were no such things as wicketkeeping coaches, it is clear that Alan Knott and Bob Taylor were not just heroes of Jack's but also massive sources of information and advice for him.

Back then we used to play teams twice. It meant that hopefully I would play against Derbyshire and Kent twice each so each time I could go and knock on the dressing room door to pick Bob and Knotty's brains because there was nobody else to help. I tried to copy Bob technically. In fact, Ian 'Gunner' Gould at Sussex used to take the Mick out of me in rain delays at Sussex [saying] that I was basically a copy of Bob, which I thought was a compliment, because if I was getting Bob's techniques right, then I mustn't have been far wrong. So, that was the basis of my game. Early on in my career I wanted to look right, because I was trying to get in the England team then. So, I was actually a bit worried about what people thought I looked like. And as you can see from the rest of my career with the state of me, I wasn't particularly bothered after a period of time. But in those early days, you try to make an impression, and at Gloucestershire to get into the England team, you had to do three times as much as everybody else. The way in was not as easy as it is now in respect of that.

As with many of your heroes, you never imagine them ever having a doubt about their game. Hearing Jack speak like this reminded me that even though I saw him as a genius, he was also a human being who had the normal fears and insecurities that all young wicketkeepers have about what others think of them. We talked about Bobby Bracey's start to his England career and how people had jumped on him immediately for not being good enough; and how we seem to have this strange critical obsession of keepers, far more than batsmen and bowlers.

> What people forget is that I actually dropped two catches on my first day in Test cricket, and one went straight through my hands off Syd Lawrence. Syd and I always talked about the dream being caught Russell bowled Lawrence and the first one that came to me was the thinnest of edges and went straight down. Knotty once told me that when you retire, you'll gain a reputation for never dropping a catch. It's like everyone forgets your mistakes and it's really true. People thought Knotty and Bob never made mistakes but obviously they did. We all do.

I mentioned to Jack that I had recently seen some old footage of him keeping wicket for Gloucestershire CCC in the 1999 C&G final. There was one particular leg-side take off the seam bowling of Mike Cawdron which is truly mind-blowing. It might actually be the best take I have ever seen. Cawdron was a medium-fast seam bowler who fired a horrible full ball a foot down the leg side. To mortal wicketkeepers, just stopping it would have been brilliant, but Jack actually took it one-handed as clean as a whistle and then promptly stood up and walked down the wicket with his chest puffed out like it was a piece of cake. It is hard to quantify the skill required to do that, other than to say that you have to be truly exceptional. I asked him what it felt like at that moment in time:

> That's the level – technical and mental. It's a combination of things but that mental state is what it is all about. Firstly, we're playing Somerset so we can't lose to them; there's no point going back down the M4 if we don't win, right? The words determination and obsession don't feel strong enough for that mental state. I had to make sure I got the job done right. A nuclear bomb could have gone off and I would still have been focused on the ball. There was nothing going to take me away from that. In fact, I tried to have this level of mindset all my career. It was a battle for me – it was me against the ball. In actual fact, that one-handed take is probably one of my best takes of my career.

And this is when we started to really drill down into the intensity that Jack brought to his wicketkeeping. There was something much more in this for me.

> Remember that there's no hiding place in our position, there's no 'let's have another go tomorrow'. I didn't want to lose, and I didn't want the ball to get past me. But just remember that this is the mindset I developed later in my career. It wasn't this good at the start; it was fifteen or twenty years in the making to get to that level. And that

feeling is like a drug. It's like a place that is almost like on another planet. It's just me against the ball. Everything else disappeared. My whole world was the ball. As the bowler started running in, the only thing I ever cared about on the planet for the next three seconds was the ball. That's the level of concentration I am talking about. In fact, and I have never told anyone this, I used to visualise a black canvas with a red ball on it. And that red ball was my life. That was my world. The batsman, the bowler, everything else was irrelevant. That's why I love painting so much because while I'm doing it, I am laser focused on it. It feels like nothing else matters in the world. It's like an escape from reality; it was the same with my keeping.

Wicketkeeping can get very technical sometimes – head position, hand position, body weight, feet position – it can go on and on. However, what Jack is talking about is nothing technical. It was all in his mind. He had an intensity of thought that created such a high level of concentration that it was bulletproof. There were so many external characteristics of Jack's that we keepers have tried to copy over the years. We could analyse how he made that extraordinary take down the leg side off Mike Cawdron from all sorts of technical viewpoints, but actually what made that bit of skill happen more than anything else was what was going on in Jack's head. He created a place of war in his mind that meant that nothing existed in his world other than him and the ball, and under no circumstances was he prepared to lose.

But the great question is how did Jack create this intensity in his mind? It would be easy to tell someone else to do this but what could we point towards to make it happen? Jack and I bounced this between us because he wasn't entirely sure himself. He had developed this mindset over years, and he was still trying to put his finger on why and how it happened. He knew it had particularly developed during the glory years for Gloucestershire in one-day cricket when John Bracewell suggested he stood up to the wickets to seam bowlers to stop batsmen leaving the crease. He knew that he and the inner ring of fielders at Gloucestershire, including the great Jonty Rhodes, had moved the 'strangle' on the batsman to another level. He knew how powerful this mindset was and knew that other elite keepers shared it. He saw it in James Foster when he took edges off full tosses or bouncers from seamers standing up when technique and mindset combined at a particular level that made that piece of skill absolutely exceptional. As we talked about this, I had a pang of regret that I hadn't found this out while playing in my professional career. For so long I had studied Jack's technique and mannerisms, but I suddenly realised that the absolute key to his brilliance was invisible.

The mindset of concentration is an interesting one for me. I get asked about concentration a lot, and I think it's an area that's a bit of a myth. We say things like 'We must concentrate hard' but we don't really know what that means. There's no set thing to concentration and everyone is a little bit different, but when I see a brilliant bit of wicketkeeping, I know they are at that level of intensity that I am talking about. I will sometimes ask young wicketkeepers if they are watching the ball. They will always reply 'Yes', but how hard are they actually watching the ball is the real question. Is it just a red blur coming at them or can they see the stitching on the seam, or what side the ball lands on? When they are keeping to a spinner are they watching the ball so hard for the last 3 feet that they can see a scratch on the ball or where it landed? That's the laser focus I am talking about. If you're not at that level of concentration then that's when something surprises you; you're not concentrating properly, you've not come prepared enough. The concentration should be in your preparation before the games. When you're at that level of concentration, nothing should surprise you. It's part of the obsession to be perfect. In fact, it is more than an obsession. I don't have the right word, but it feels stronger than an obsession.

My whole life was geared around catching a ball. I walked past my wife one day as she was stood by the gate at Bristol. There were only about three people there and I didn't even see her because all I was focused on was what I needed to do to be ready for 11 am the next day. I've talked about it in my own book, but I even missed my grandmother's funeral. I'm not proud of it but I'd forgotten all about it because all I was thinking about was my cricket.

It was just fascinating to hear Jack talk like this. That burning fire of intensity around his wicketkeeping was unquestionable, but what lit the fire? It definitely came from an emotionalisation of what his role was, and I want to explain this as clearly as I can. Jack reached that level of intensity because he emotionalised the outcome or the battle that he was involved in to such an incredible extent that he felt like he had no other purpose on the earth other than to get this right; and the 'this' was his wicketkeeping at that moment in time. Emotionalisation arises from two things – the thought of being brilliant or the thought of not wanting to make a mistake. This relates to the theory or belief that all men are motivated by fear or greed. I have already referred back to the C&G final that I played at Lord's in 2006 with Lancashire, in which my overriding thought was, 'Don't fuck up.' I kept perfectly that day. The emotionalisation of what mistakes would mean drove me to not make a single one with the gloves. In fact, I believe that 99.9 per cent of my career was driven by that emotionalisation. Geraint Jones shared the same drive based on fear of not messing up, whereas the likes of Chris Read and Sarah Taylor seemed to find their drive from the confidence they had in that they could show the world how brilliant they were. So, where did Jack sit in this spectrum?

> I'm with you. I'm with you. When I first started playing and I wanted to get into the England team, nobody would notice anyone down at Bristol because everything was dominated by the Home Counties back then. But each ground would have a reporter from the *Telegraph*, and it used to help me focus and concentrate that I did not want to see in the newspaper next day 'Russell dropped so and so'. I used it as my driving force. I would just think about how pissed off I would be at the end of the day's play, sat in the changing room, knowing I've missed one. I don't want that. I don't want to be angry and pissed off all night because I haven't concentrated properly. I want to know I've done a good job that day … that I haven't missed anything. So, what you're saying about

your thoughts when you were walking out at Lord's is very natural to me. I was the same. I was driven by not wanting to make a mistake. I hear people saying you've got to 'enjoy the day' when you play in a Lord's final. Well, that's not for me, because I think I might get a bit slack. At the end of the day's play, if we're lifting up the cup and I've not made a mistake then I can enjoy it. In fact, then I will enjoy it for the rest of my life, but not before that.

This look into the mindset that helped make Jack a truly exceptional wicketkeeper was incredible for me. For years, I had almost apologised in my mind for the fact that my entire cricket career was driven by a fear of failure. If I am honest, I thought it was a weakness of mine. I perceived in my mind that the 'greats' never thought like this. I presumed that they were always driven by the fact that they would have a stage to show everyone how good they were while I was driven by not wanting to let everyone down. Yet here was my wicketkeeping hero telling me that he shared my mindset and had used it to light a ferocious fire of intensity that could take him to an extremely high level of concentration, focus and, therefore, performance. All of this actually challenges many of the ways that we handle and coach young keepers. It puts a different slant on the 'think positive' mantra. Jack shows that your emotions are an incredibly powerful force in driving your performance so it is not a case of telling someone how they should feel but rather helping them channel that emotion into something that will drive their performance.

Much of this chapter and my chat with Jack was focused on mindset because that was the biggest area that I wanted to dig into but it would be remiss of me to imply that Jack's wicketkeeping standards were solely driven by this. It clearly had a huge effect on his performance but, as Jack points out, there are other attributes:

> You've got to have a certain physique to do it. But I don't think that's set in stone because you've got big and small keepers that can do it. So, I don't think there's a given, but agility is a key one, as well as hand-to-eye coordination. I think I might've been born with that because if I drop a cup then I can catch it.

It is also true to say that Jack was a brilliant technical wicketkeeper. His body, head and hand positions were outstanding. As with all true greats, they are a perfect combination of technical, physical and mindset attributes. But the interesting part of this is what made Jack *that* much better than everyone else and I truly believe it was his mindset. He brought a level of intensity to wicketkeeping that placed him in a mental state that created exceptional performances. I go back to that leg-side take off Mike Cawdron in the C&G final – that piece of skill and his look afterwards were of a wicketkeeper at war, with determination to win against the ball at all costs.

I talked at the start of the book about the fact that I believe the phrase a 'keepers' keeper' is overused in the game and is often said when someone simply looks like what someone else feels a keeper should look like. It's used as an external or aesthetic reference more than anything else. Jack looked like a keeper in many people's eyes with his hat, gloves and pads, so they wanted other keepers to look like him; otherwise they weren't 'true' keepers. As Jack has himself said, keepers come in all shapes and sizes, so I believe that phrase is more often than not used in the wrong context. However, Sarah Taylor pointed out to me that there are wicketkeepers for whom the role is more than a job – it is an absolute obsession that comes from deep within. For Sarah, it is her happy place in the world which made her feel that she was born to be a wicketkeeper and I entirely believe her. So, what does Jack tell me about what it is to be a true keeper or a keepers' keeper, or however anyone wants to phrase it?

> I get asked my opinion on keepers a lot – shall we sign someone etc. I have been to Academy trials and done some scouting. The very first question I asked all young keepers is, 'Do you love it?' Because if they truly love it, then they've got a good chance, because that means they'll be able to take the knocks and they'll come back for more. They get knocked down and they'll get up. There has to be a love for it – that obsession, that determination that basically your life revolves around catching a ball.

And, I think, there it is.

To be a true wicketkeeper it has to be the most important thing that happens for you on a cricket field. And, at times, it might just have to be the most important thing that happens for you in life. Your burning obsession with it comes from somewhere deep in your soul that drives you through brick walls to try to do it perfectly every single day of your career. It is you against the ball, and nothing else matters, ball after ball after ball. You will think about it day and night, and constantly strive for greater

Celebrating taking a catch for Lancashire during a County Championship match against Somerset in 2008.

Jos Buttler, arguably one of the most talented cricketers ever produced by England, during the Second Test match against Pakistan, August 2020.

Geraint Jones was involved in some of the greatest Test matches in English cricket history. Here he stands ready behind the stumps for the First Test against Pakistan at Lord's, 2006.

Chris Read looks on as Andy Bichel sweeps the ball for Essex in 2007. In my eyes, Chris was one of the purest wicketkeepers of my era.

Sarah Taylor set new standards for the women's game and was described by Adam Gilchrist in 2018 as the best wicketkeeper in the world, male or female. Here she appeals for the wicket of Grace Harris during the Women's Ashes NatWest T20, in 2015.

Jack Russell was the reason I wanted to be a wicketkeeper. For me, he's the Wicketkeeping King.

'The Gaffer', Alec Stewart, was one of my cricketing idols. A true England cricketing legend.

Warren Hegg was the heartbeat of any Lancashire side who took to the field, and always speaks with energy and passion about his love for the art of wicketkeeping.

Future England coach Peter Moores keeping wicket for Sussex in 1992. There is no one in the world of cricket that I respect more than him.

Michael Bates has been described as a 'true wicketkeeper', both as a player and as a coach. This photograph was taken during Hampshire's T20 Final victory against Somerset in 2010.

Amy Jones keeping wicket for England during the Third T20 against India, July 2021. Her connection with the energy required to be a keeper has led her to be one of the world's best.

Keith Piper had a natural brilliance behind the stumps and was mentioned in glowing terms by everyone I spoke to. Here he is celebrating the wicket of Graeme Hick, who had just been bowled first ball for 0.

perfection. You will know that others don't really understand or maybe even appreciate what you do, and you will know that you will experience physical pain, but you don't care because it is you against the ball and that is all that matters.

When people use the phrase 'keepers' keeper' in passing positive or negative judgement on a wicketkeeper then they should forget appearance, mannerisms, size, technique or style and they should solely refer to what I have said above because that's who Jack was on the cricket field and that's why he was so extraordinarily brilliant with the gloves.

I wanted this chapter to go on forever because Jack brought so much to this book.

The Wicketkeeping King.

JACK RUSSELL CAREER AVERAGES

| Batting & Fielding | | | | | | | | | | |
Format	Matches	Innings	Runs	HS	Ave	SR	100s	50s	Ct	St
Test	54	86	1897	128*	27.1	35.86	2	6	153	12
ODI	40	31	423	50	17.62	66.3	0	1	41	6
FC	465	690	16861	129*	30.93	–	11	89	1192	128
List A	479	367	6626	119*	24.09	–	2	25	465	98
T20	2	1	11	11*	–	220	0	0	1	1

Chapter 8

Warren Hegg

A t the end of the 2005 season, I left Derbyshire CCC to join Lancashire CCC. I know this will upset a few Derbyshire supporters, but the truth is that there are not too many bigger jumps in county cricket. In fact, I have one story that sums up just how big a move this was for me.

I arrived in Manchester in November 2005 having found a new home in Didsbury, a lovely part of the south region of the city. I was nervous and excited to get started with Lancashire and joined up immediately with the squad for winter training. In my very first training session in the indoor centre at Old Trafford, Freddie Flintoff was there. He wasn't training himself but had just popped in to say hello to the lads. I actually knew Freddie pretty well because we are only about a year apart in age and had played a fair bit of junior cricket with each other. However, if I am completely honest, I was a bit star-struck when I saw him at the time. England had just beaten Australia in 'that' 2005 Ashes series and Freddie's profile was gigantic. He wasn't just a cricket star; he was an enormous personality in both sport and entertainment. He was moving the dial as to what was possible for a cricketer in every way, living in a completely different world to 99.9 per cent of other professional cricketers. He greeted me and everyone else in his usual big hugging way without there being an ounce of him being anything other than the normal 'Freddie'. He told me that he had a benefit dinner that night at Old Trafford Football Ground and that I should come along and be on the table with some of the other Lancashire lads who would be there. A benefit year is granted to a cricketer as a fundraiser for him and his chosen charities as a thank you for his services to that club, and that year at Lancashire was dedicated to Freddie. I was keen to fit in and get to know everyone, so I quickly accepted the invitation. Strangely enough, I was also due to attend another benefit dinner the following evening for Derbyshire's Kevin Dean.

So that evening I got suited and booted and headed off to the 'Theatre of Dreams' to meet the other lads for Freddie's dinner. It began with a VIP drinks reception and my jaw literally hit the floor when I walked in – it was like the Who's Who of elite sport in the North West. Sir Alex Ferguson, Ryan Giggs, Sam Allardyce and Lee Westwood were just a few of the big names there. And these people weren't there reluctantly; they *wanted* to be there and be associated with Freddie. The whole night was huge in every way – the number of people, the celebrities, the excitement, the entertainment and, of course, the money spent. It was something that I had never experienced before. Incidentally, we were on a table on one far side of the massive room, which was absolutely fine but, as Lancashire county cricketers, we were definitely not the star attractions that night!

The following night I headed back to Derby for Kevin Dean's benefit dinner. Kevin was an extremely worthy recipient of a benefit year as a brilliant bloke and player for the club. He had devoted his entire career to the club and had performed brilliantly over many years. Anyway (and I hate saying this as someone who loved everything about Derbyshire), the difference between the two evenings couldn't have been starker. Kevin's was held in the

Derbyshire CCC pavilion for about 120 people versus Freddie's 1,500 people in one of the biggest hospitality suites in a world-famous football ground. But more than anything, it was the difference in the VIP guests: to match Sir Alex Ferguson, Kevin had ... guess who? ME! I was introduced to everyone as the main VIP on the night. It was very flattering but big fish in small pond ... yeah, all that in spades.

This is obviously just about benefit dinners and maybe not an entirely fair comparison bearing in mind Freddie's world dwarfed almost everyone else's at that time, but the difference in the clubs was apparent in every way – numbers of supporters, size of grounds, facilities, expectations, pressure and, of course, quality of players. I remember looking around the Lancashire dressing room and just seeing a load of world-class players. And this point on the quality of players was never lost on me with regards to the man I was taking over from with the gloves at Lancashire – Warren Hegg. Warren was someone whom I had admired for years and I was probably a bit in awe of. He was an outstanding wicketkeeper who was equally as brilliant keeping to Wasim Akram as he was Muttiah Muralitharan. Having those two as overseas players at Lancashire meant that the club could showcase the breadth of Warren's ability as a wicketkeeper – he was right up there with the very best. He was also the heartbeat of any Lancashire side that took the field, so I was well aware of the weight of responsibility I was taking on in replacing him. I certainly felt a pressure in my mind to live up to the standards that he had set over a very long career.

Warren was from an era of great wicketkeepers in county cricket that could all have played for England individually. The likes of Steve Rhodes, Colin Metson, Richard Blakey, Keith

Piper, Karl Krikken, Rob Turner and Bruce French were all outstanding and, remarkably, all sat behind Jack Russell and Alec Stewart. With this in mind, when I spoke to him, Warren remarked:

> Yeah, it was red-hot competition back then and it was always you against the opposition keeper. If I could dominate the opposition keeper then I knew that I was doing my job for the team. And if you look at the keepers then – of course, there was Jack Russell and Alec Stewart, who we all wanted to knock off the top, but there were lesser names who were also brilliant. Adrian Aymes at Hampshire was excellent, as was Bobby Parks, who was before him. There was just quality everywhere. It felt like we were all competing to be the understudy on tour to Jack or Alec.

That generation of wicketkeepers were the guys one ahead of my time. They set a ferocious standard for wicketkeeping in England which we all felt we had to live with. Chris Read talked about that being a big driver in his motivation to being considered as one of the best. He wanted to be talked about in the same bracket as the likes of Warren Hegg. The fact that in the end Warren went on three full England tours and made his international debut in Australia says a lot about how good he really was during that era.

I have spoken to Warren about wicketkeeping a lot over the years and every time I do, his face lights up. He talks with an energy and passion that can't hide his deep love for the art.

From the very first time I tried wicketkeeping, I just became besotted with it. I remember closely watching the first team wicketkeeper at my club back then, Stand CC in Whitefield, who was called Derek Bickley. Derek had trials at Derbyshire and was a great keeper. He was left-handed so going down the leg side looked so natural for him and he stood up to all the seam bowlers and took some amazing leg-side stumpings. It was beautiful to watch. I studied him, I mean absolutely studied everything he did – from the way he caught the ball, the way he crouched down, the way he collected the ball from the outfield – and I became a real wicketkeeping nerd. That's all I wanted to do, and batting became secondary. I wanted to stand up to everyone and get as many stumpings and catches as I could. That love of wicketkeeping was there then and is here now just as much.

Warren talked in exactly the same way as Sarah Taylor about how it was love at first try with wicketkeeping – almost like they were born to do it and had found one of their great passions in life. But Warren also spoke with the same burning intensity as Jack Russell about the mindset of a wicketkeeper. This was always going to be more than just a job for Warren:

It's an obsession. I think wicketkeepers have to be slightly obsessive in their character. I don't think you can be laid back. I've got slight OCD. If I'm going to do something, then I want to do it right. I want to do it perfectly, which is what us keepers are trying to do every day – be perfect. If I do something wrong then I beat myself up and that's in anything, not just keeping. But I think those characteristics are in all wicketkeepers. This included my kit – I had a scalpel and a sewing kit and while we were batting, I would repair my gloves because they needed to be right. They needed to perfect. It really is an obsession.

I think Warren's right on this. I am an obsessive character, which is my greatest strength and greatest weakness in life, all wrapped up in one. That ability to hyperfocus pushes you to search for perfection in everything you do, but equally, it can create demons in your head when you don't get it right. As I've said publicly before, it's like challenging yourself to draw a straight line without something to help you like a ruler or a guide: how long can you go in trying to make that perfectly straight? The answer … forever; and it could drive you mad! Warren's correct – it's that intensity that real wicketkeepers have for the role and the reason they completely submerge themselves in the art along with everything it brings, both good and bad.

I still get wicketkeeping dreams. In fact, I had one the other night. In my dream, I don't know where I'm keeping, but someone nicks it. I can see the ball perfectly and feel good. It's a catch that I've caught a hundred times and then I move to catch it … sometimes I catch it, sometimes I don't; I drop it. I just jump up and move in bed and wake my wife up. She thinks I'm bloody mad!

Warren battled as hard as anyone for international recognition and when he was picked for the 2001/2 England tours to India and New Zealand alongside James Foster, he looked an excellent chance to play. Foster was young and untried, and Warren had the game to do well in the tough conditions of India. Unfortunately, he just carried the drinks all tour as he watched Foster struggle most of the series.

> I really thought I would play in India. My batting, with my sweeps and use of my feet, could do well out there, but Duncan Fletcher was building his team and wanted Foster in there. It was a tough one, but I had to accept it.

After Foster's tough time in India, most felt Warren would get a shot in New Zealand, but it wasn't to be. Foster was again preferred by Fletcher. That was effectively the end of Warren's international chances. Despite those sorts of bitter disappointments, it is quite clear that nothing has ever diminished from Warren's deep passion for wicketkeeping. It is the centre of his focus within cricket and he empathises with every keeper out there. It is definitely with his community of men and women that he feels most at home.

> A couple of years ago, I was invited to an MCC dinner at Lord's for all living international wicketkeepers. It was amazing. There were twenty-five wicketkeeping badgers in one room. It was brilliant! So, there were all the living wicketkeepers who had kept for England plus ten to twelve legendary keepers – the likes of Derek Murray, Farokh Engineer, Rod Marsh, Ian Healy and Wasim Bari. And it was the most amazing, surreal experience I have been in. I remember sitting with Farokh Engineer,

Bob Taylor, Jeff Dujon and Derek Murray talking about wicketkeeping in one of the hotels in London. It was like a wicketkeeping badgers' convention! I just sat there and thought, you know, this is absolutely incredible. You couldn't pay enough money to be able to sit in this room and listen to these blokes talk about their experiences and all their funny stories. And that love of wicketkeeping was in everyone there; it was amazing.

This book was very much about trying to give people an insight into the world of wicketkeeping through the lenses of the very best who have done it in this country. Warren was doing this for me without even talking about his own wicketkeeping, which I found incredible. He was reminding me what a brother and sisterhood the wicketkeeping community really was. Ask this question – do batsmen meet up and feel that sense of community as Warren did with the other keepers at Lord's? I don't believe so.

I don't like seeing any keeper struggle. It pains me. Like Bracey at Lord's on his debut. It was tough for him, but my heart went out to him as I knew he didn't quite have the experience to deal with that moment. I just want to see all keepers do well.

There was so much that Warren said that overlapped with what others said within this book, but he really did give me this extra dimension to what the 'Keepers' Union' really means. Now, if this was a way to judge who was a 'keepers' keeper' then there's no question in my mind that Warren qualified for it wholeheartedly. But I didn't want to get too far away from

Warren's own experiences because he really was an exceptional wicketkeeper. I asked him if he ever remembered a moment when he was right at the top of his game with the gloves.

> I remember we played Somerset at Old Trafford in the 1990 Benson & Hedges semi-final. We were a bloody good team then but so were Somerset. They had the South African Jimmy Cook playing for them – he was a brilliant player, smashing it everywhere. Before the game, I felt brilliant, like I was catching pigeons. Just before lunch, Phil DeFreitas bounced Richard Harden and he gloves it down the leg side. I remember taking off down the leg side and pulling this thing out of the air one-handed and at pace; and I just remember thinking, 'That's unbelievable, how have you caught that?' And then about half an hour after lunch, Jimmy Cook was facing Ian Austin and he went on the back foot to cut a ball too close to him. He cut it and it went up and to my right. I knew immediately that it was a very tough catch and if I wasn't at my absolute best it would get away from me. I dived and caught it with two hands, and I think most people would have thought it was a regulation catch. It wasn't, though it was a great catch that I made look easy. And in those moments, everything just felt natural. Completely natural. I wasn't thinking about feet or hand position, just catching the ball. I just focused on that ball and that's all that mattered.

That last sentence was very much Warren echoing what Jack Russell had said – all that mattered was the ball.

Warren played in many one-day finals with brilliant Lancashire sides in the 1990s and I told him about my 'don't fuck up' mindset in my one-day final for Lancashire back in 2006. I wanted to know if fear ever dictated to him like that or whether he was solely focused on showing everyone how brilliant he was.

> That's a really good question. If I'm honest, I think I had a bit of both, but I think that mindset you are describing is completely natural. Even when you are at the top of your game, you have that feeling in your belly about not making a mistake. I'll throw it back to our Benson & Hedges cup final in 1990 against Worcestershire. Now we were a brilliant side then but Worcestershire, with Hick, Curtis, Newport etc., were also excellent. In the whole build-up to the game, it was all about Akram versus Hick. Two world-class players and whoever came out on top in that mini battle might just dictate the end result. Akram v Hick all the way to the final. And I remember thinking again and again, 'What if I drop Hick off Akram? What will everyone think?' There was all this build-up between the two of them and it just heightened it for me on my possible role in that battle. Anyway ... guess what happened? Hick was bowled Akram, caught Hegg, and we won the game. That fear didn't drive me to make a mistake. In fact, I nailed it.

The wonderful thing about writing this book was that every wicketkeeper I spoke to seemed to give me a slightly different angle to consider as to what being a wicketkeeper was all about. I loved how Warren had this huge connection to fellow wicketkeepers. As a self-confessed 'wicketkeeping nerd', he has a massive appreciation for other wicketkeepers – what they go through and the beauty of the skill that they deliver. The funny thing about this is that I spent years trying to live up to his standards at Lancashire and was desperate for his approval as my predecessor, but what I have discovered is that Warren will root for every wicketkeeper out there, and likely did for me back in the day.

Warren was an exceptional gloveman and embodied so much of what people would consider to be a true wicketkeeper – his ability, his size, his look and his spirit. But maybe over the top of all of that is his sense of community with wicketkeeping – it's where he truly feels at home in the game. He told me a story about when he helped catch the ball in warm-ups for the Lancashire bowlers prior to a game. This is something normally done with a baseball catching glove.

> I thought, 'Sod it; I'm putting some wicketkeeping gloves on to do it.' It felt better and I wanted to catch a few again. I started trying some of the new catching techniques, where you catch the ball further out in front of you. You know what? I really liked it. I could have done that back in the day.

As he told me this, I could see his face lighting up again as his mind ticked over about wicketkeeping and new techniques.

And that's it – Warren is a true wicketkeeper. He feels at home talking about it, studying it, practising it and performing it, and even more so with fellow keepers.

Just maybe, he was born to do it.

WARREN HEGG CAREER AVERAGES

| Batting & Fielding | | | | | | | | | |
Format	Matches	Innings	Runs	HS	Ave	SR	100s	50s	Ct	St
Test	2	4	30	15	7.5	34.88	0	0	8	0
FC	348	504	11302	134	27.9	–	7	55	857	94
List A	409	245	3313	81	19.95	–	0	5	466	61
T20	20	13	104	45	11.55	97.19	0	0	10	8

Chapter 9

Alec Stewart

Ok, time for full disclosure.

I have already mentioned what a massive influence Jack Russell had on me wanting to be a wicketkeeper, but a player whom I held in absolute awe was Alec Stewart. I loved him as a cricketer for England.

It was tough during the 1990s to watch the England cricket team. The team changed a lot and we really struggled against the best in the world – forty-three defeats versus twenty-six wins in that decade said it all. But the thing I used to find the hardest to watch was our fragility. The West Indians and, particularly, the Australians just seemed to dominate us in every sense. I hate to say it, but it felt like we were bullied at times. But Alec was different. He was brilliantly talented, but he also took it to the opposition. He didn't wait to be dominated; he tried to impose himself immediately on a game. With the constant twirling of his bat and lifting up of his shirt collars, you always felt like he was up for a battle. Of course, this applied to his batting, with his deep-in-the-crease attacking style, but it also applied to him as a personality and, eventually, as a full-time international wicketkeeper. I always remember watching Alec and thinking that he was the sort of person that I wanted representing the Three Lions.

Since my retirement from professional cricket I have got to know Alec fairly well and never actually disclosed my fan-boy status to him (until now!). I have one distinct memory that summed up how in awe I always was of Alec. In 1998, I was in the British Universities side that played in the Benson & Hedges Cup. It was back in the day when the universities could pick a combined best XI and would have a place in the group stages of the competition. In my year, we had a pretty decent side captained by ex-Warwickshire Anurag Singh. We very nearly beat Hampshire at the Parks and Somerset at Taunton; and we actually did beat Gloucestershire at Bristol by 7 runs! By the way, that was a Gloucestershire side that included Courtney Walsh, Jack Russell and Mark Alleyne. Let it be whispered that a 39 runs off thirty-five balls partnership at the end of our innings between L. Sutton and A. Strauss might have helped! One of our other group games was against Surrey at The Oval in which A. Stewart featured on the opposition scorecard. In fact, he was wicketkeeping in this game.

I genuinely idolised Alec so just being on the same field as him was a big deal for me. When I batted in that game, the leg spinner Iain Salisbury came on to bowl. Strangely enough, Iain and I ended up playing at the same club in Australia a couple of years later and became great friends, but at this point, we didn't know each other. As I took guard I could see Alec and did my best to stay composed. Iain tossed up a fullish ball outside the off stump and I drove it through the covers for four. As I hit the ball and from behind the stumps, Alec said, 'Shot', as in good shot! One of my genuine heroes has just said good shot to me while I was playing against him! I didn't know what to do with myself. As I ran down the wicket, I nearly tripped over my feet as I tried to look back to see if he had really said that. I was so overawed by it that I just got running after the ball had crossed the boundary and needed my batting partner to tell me to stop! Thankfully, no one was really paying attention to me at the time, but it would have been a very embarrassing sight. Saying that, I am now very embarrassed knowing that Alec is reading this!

Obviously I followed Alec's career very closely. His hundreds in both innings in his 100th Test against the West Indies crowned him as a total legend, but throughout his career, I also studied his wicketkeeping. This was partly because I was a wicketkeeper myself but also because Jack was a hero of mine, so the debate over who should have the gloves in the England team was one that I was fully invested in. The truth is that I was completely torn with it and for the majority of the time sat firmly on the fence. What I can say, though, is that Alec became an outstanding wicketkeeper for England. It feels a disservice to choose a particular catch or stumping of his to illustrate this point, but I will never forget his low, left- and one-handed catch of Brian Lara off Darren Gough at Lord's – it was as good as it gets, standing back. It was low, fast and to his weaker side, which meant that everything needed to be perfect technically, which it was.

Hero status apart, Alec was a must for this book. The reason for that is he was the archetypal batsman who was asked to become a wicketkeeper, who then became an outstanding wicketkeeper. Of all the nonsense that we hear in the game about what makes a great keeper and what they should look like, Alec's own personal journey within this was always going to be an outstanding insight because he started so late in his career to give it serious focus.

When I signed for Surrey, they signed me as a batsman who could possibly keep. It wasn't really until I went to Perth in Australia to play for Midland Guildford when

I went as a batsman-keeper. It was my first winter away and I was just 18 years old. I was starting out in my professional career and at Midland Guildford I started to really learn to keep wicket. I kept a little bit with Surrey when I was in my mid-twenties, but Jack Richards was our keeper and I got in the first team as a number 3 or number 4 batter. I actually made my first-team debut at Cheltenham as a keeper, when Jack had bust a finger. But it wasn't until 1996/7 when I went to Zimbabwe and New Zealand with England, and Bumble and Athers were in charge, that things seriously changed for me with my wicketkeeping. Jack was on the tour but when we met up at the Gatwick Airport Hotel they called me into the room at the hotel and said, 'We're looking at you to be our number 1 keeper.' I said, 'No problem,' but the last thing I wanted to do was drop down the order. So, I batted at 3 on that tour and kept wicket. And it's the first time I really started thinking very much as a batsman-wicketkeeper. I gave far more work to my keeping than perhaps I had previously. Before then I was probably 65/35 on focusing on my batting and keeping at practice. Once they said that, it became very much 50/50. I gave much more time to specific keeping practice to make sure I was at a good enough level to keep in international cricket regularly.

To put some context into this, at this stage in Alec's career he had already been playing international cricket for seven years and was an outstanding batsman. To suddenly turn the switch on to 'thinking like a keeper' and then become so excellent really goes against the old adage that you are born a wicketkeeper. There has always been this mystique around what it meant to think like a true keeper but for Alec it was pretty simple:

> It was just the way I applied myself in training. That was all. So, whereas before it was my batting that was a priority and I made sure my fielding was up to standard, but then when I became the number 1 England keeper in 1996–7, the fielding went out the window and it was very much 50/50 on batting and keeping.

The romanticism of wicketkeepers of yesteryear means that people still have this obsession that keepers are these eccentric oddballs who were destined to be keepers from the moment they were born, but Alec was the purest example of the opposite of this, even back in the 1990s. Like I've said a few times already, Alec was an outstanding international wicketkeeper.

> Bob Taylor wasn't eccentric in my opinion. He was a purist. Alan Knott was but I definitely wouldn't say Bob was. And just thinking now around the current county cricket and national wicketkeepers, I've not seen too many who are off the wall, to be honest, no. For me, it's about working hard. It's been about being the best you can be by working hard and enjoying it. Don't get me wrong, you've got to enjoy it – that's the most important thing. But I don't see that characteristic of keepers being different in the current game.

It's impossible to look back on Alec as an England wicketkeeper without also thinking of Jack Russell. Their careers ran alongside each other and they each perfectly represented the changing role of the wicketkeeper as we approached the millennium. I had spoken to Jack before I spoke to Alec and I found the contrast between them absolutely fascinating. Aesthetically they couldn't have been more different – Jack as the scruffy, eccentric one and Alec as the smart, polished one. But I discovered that the differences went far beyond just their physical appearances. When Jack talked about what made a great wicketkeeper, he talked almost exclusively about the mind, whereas for Alec, it was a different focus:

> You've got to be strong in your hips and legs so you're agile and can move well. You need good concentration. And then it's about your hands; you need fast hands and reaction time, like a Ben Foakes. You need those sorts of hands where the ball just melts into your gloves, like Keith Piper back in the day.

Both Jack and Alec acknowledged that you have to love the role to do it successfully but for Jack the emphasis was on loving 'being a wicketkeeper' – almost a persona type of thing – whereas for Alec it was much more about loving the role so that you are prepared to put in the necessary work. Alec's most current reference of this is Ben Foakes, who is describes as the best keeper in the world at the moment.

> I have obviously worked a lot with Foakesy and at times I have to tell him to stop with his practice because he would do his drills all day long and burn himself out.

Thankfully he's now backed off it a bit because he would be doing so much, almost too much. So come game day, he could be a bit fatigued. So, I have said to him, 'We're only going to do twenty minutes' practice today, not forty-five minutes', and I promise you, you won't be a worse keeper for it.' That's the intensity within the make-up of a top keeper. As a coach I don't want to be dragging my keeper onto the field to do some practice.

Another massive difference between the two of them was their mindset with regards to performing. As I've already explained, Jack was driven by a fierce determination not to make a mistake. His laser focus was based on his emotionalisation of the consequences of making mistakes – similar to my 'don't fuck up' mindset in my C&G final for Lancashire against Sussex in 2006. Once again, Alec was the polar opposite of this.

Once I was confident in my keeping ability, I actually wanted to show off how good I was. I don't want that to sound big-headed, but that's where it got to. There is that question of would you prefer to do it in front of 100,000 or 1,000 people? I would always take 100,000 people. The bigger the occasion, the bigger the atmosphere; the more people watching, the more it drove me on.

These were two wicketkeepers of the same era who reached exceptional standards on the international scene and who couldn't have been more different in background, appearance and mindset. If ever anyone needed proof that the wicketkeeping community is a big tent, then this was it.

There is no doubt, however, that Alec shares the same frustration as every wicketkeeper I have so far talked about in this book – the amount of misunderstanding out there about what the role of the wicketkeeper actually means.

> Wicketkeeping is a specialist position so people see you with the gloves on and believe you should catch every ball. It's the same as goalkeepers. A keeper might take a worldly catch but if he or she's dropped one, it will gain much more attention, especially on social media nowadays. In my opinion, the keeper dropping a catch shouldn't be any different to a first slip or mid-off dropping one or mid-off drop. It's a chance that should be taken but it doesn't make it any different if you're a keeper or a fielder. So, keepers have to be really thick-skinned and mentally strong. You are also meant to be that person in the team – a cheerleader, keeping the troops going and all those things. So, responsibility comes with being a keeper and unless you've done the job, you won't understand it. People just think you put on a pair of gloves and it's easy. That's why I think that the 'Keepers Union' is a real thing. We all understand what we've been through – the tough times, what you have to put up with and the jobs you have to do. And that's why I think it is a unique club of people.

It's widely acknowledged with the cricketing fraternity that Adam Gilchrist was a game changer for the role of wicketkeeper. In short, every team wanted one of him – an accomplished wicketkeeper who could walk out to bat at 7 and change the tempo of the game singlehandedly. It's ultimately why Geraint Jones was picked ahead of Chris Read and Matt Prior over James Foster. This evolution or movement triggered the debate about whether the pure art of wicketkeeping was being lost. People felt that batsmen were being crudely converted into wicketkeepers. Phrases like 'He's not a keepers' keeper' were banded about as some people saw their romantic vision of the wicketkeeper being tarnished. Indeed, within this book, we have seen differing views about this amongst our wicketkeepers. Sarah Taylor disclosed that she felt you were born to be a wicketkeeper; you couldn't be made into one. To this day, this debate lives strong over whether the England Test team should include Ben Foakes or Jos Buttler. Some people feel so strongly about this that they almost see the whole thing as an affront to the great history of wicketkeeping within this country. Alec Stewart provides the biggest antidote to this argument. I don't think he was born to be a wicketkeeper. In fact, he was a fairly reluctant wicketkeeper in the early part of his professional career, let alone when he was a teenager. He considered himself as a temporary wicketkeeper all the way up until he had that conversation with David Lloyd and Michael Atherton at a hotel in Gatwick Airport in 1996. From that moment, a switch turned on inside him that would mean he would work extremely hard to be the best wicketkeeper he could be because his country needed him to be. This was combined with a deep pride in his performances that meant he would do whatever was necessary to be an excellent international wicketkeeper – and he achieved exactly that.

Now some might say to me, 'Alec was good, but he was no Jack Russell or Ian Healy behind the stumps,' in order to pull the argument back to the fact that someone can't be made into a 'true' wicketkeeper. Well, I have a couple of points to make on this. Firstly, Alec was as good as Jack and Healy for long periods of his career. I would even argue that, standing back, he was better than Jack at certain times. He was an outstanding international wicketkeeper. As a side note to this point, Jos Buttler's keeping in England's recent tours to Sri Lanka and India was as good as anyone's. Secondly, this whole argument can't hang on whether someone is better than someone else. Those debates constantly rage on in all sport. This has to be about whether someone is able to reach a standard that makes them excellent on the international stage. There is no doubt that Alec did that.

I asked Alec if he had periods in his career that he really 'felt' like a keeper.

Yeah, it's just rhythm. You don't have to think; you just do it. Now, you obviously concentrate and fully focus, but it just feels easy. The opposite is like when you're out of sync when batting, you're thinking about everything else apart from the ball. By the time you realise that, the ball is rushing you and it's the same when you're keeping. If you feel comfortable in your stance, your movements, the balls are going into your hands nicely; all you do is focus on the ball.

What I find really fascinating about his reply is actually what he didn't say. He didn't talk about feeling part of an unusual group of cricketers with strange mannerisms and the kit looking, feeling and even smelling a certain way. His answer was simple, matter-of-fact stuff, and interestingly, he compared it to batting.

There were no hidden wicketkeeping nuances to reveal; it was just simple cricket talk about how you feel when you're playing well as a wicketkeeper and, indeed, as a batsman. Through some of the misinformed and romantic nonsense we hear in the commentary of the modern wicketkeeper, this from Alec cuts through it all.

Alec Stewart is a true England cricketing legend and someone whom I absolutely idolised as a youngster with dreams of being a professional cricketer. His playing career, and now as a coach, tells us so much about how wicketkeepers can be developed up to the highest level. His insight is definitely not to be ignored.

Just maybe, being an excellent wicketkeeper is about dedicating yourself to the role and work involved more than strange cricketing quirks.

ALEC STEWART CAREER AVERAGES

Batting & Fielding										
Format	Matches	Innings	Runs	HS	Ave	SR	100s	50s	Ct	St
Test	133	235	8463	190	39.54	48.66	15	45	263	14
ODI	170	162	4677	116	31.6	68.36	4	28	159	15
FC	447	734	26165	271*	40.06	–	48	148	721	32
List A	504	474	14771	167*	35.08	–	19	94	442	48

Chapter 10

Amy Jones

'Wicketkeepers are the players most engaged in the game.'

I got something different from every wicketkeeper I spoke to for this book – whether it was about their approach to the role or what they saw in other wicketkeepers. Amy Jones was no different and this sentence from her was one that really stuck with me. I will come back to it.

With over 100 England caps to her name, Amy is no newbie to international cricket. Yet, it is only recently that it feels like she has completely risen out of the shadow of Sarah Taylor. Taylor was an outstanding wicketkeeper for England who set new standards for the women's game – she was certainly a hard act to follow. But Amy's path in doing so was very much transitional rather than the grand exchange of the number 1 England wicketkeeper baton! In fact, when Taylor retired in 2019, Amy had already kept wicket in forty-two of her eighty England matches across all formats at that moment in time.

'To be honest,' she said, 'it really helped me. I was kind of filtered into the team. Before Sarah had officially stepped away and I knew it was my role, I was sort of doing it already.'

Despite this, it is clear that Amy's journey towards creating her own reputation as a top international wicketkeeper has needed a few jolts of energy. In an interview in early 2021 with Nick Friend at *The Cricketer*, Amy opened up about sliding into a comfort zone of being in Taylor's shadow but then how the shock of missing out on the 2017 World Cup helped her see beyond that.

> Because of my keeping, I was quickly put into the squad as number 2. So I think I quickly got used to running the drinks and being really chuffed just to be on tour. Obviously, I was playing with some brilliant players who I'd grown up watching on the telly and going down to support. So, I think it felt pretty surreal almost for too long. I was in that phase of thinking, 'Wow, this is cool – I'm so lucky to be here.' I was in that phase for far too long, looking back. I think every player has that moment where you pinch yourself because you're in a dressing room with the likes of Katherine Brunt, Sarah Taylor, Laura Marsh, Lydia Greenway and Charlotte Edwards. But ideally you don't want to be in that phase for too long. You want to feel like you should be there and like you deserve to be there, and I guess that only properly came for me after having the big setback of the World Cup and realising that I wasn't 19 anymore.

The theme of energy kept coming back around as I spoke to Amy about wicketkeeping, and this was not a physical energy but more a passion and engagement type of energy. It was becoming increasingly clear to me that this is how Amy has developed as a cricketer but particularly as a wicketkeeper. To go alongside her statement at the start of this chapter, she also describes wicketkeepers as 'very invested in the game'. She speaks of Michael Bates in glowing terms, as Sarah Taylor did, and how his passion and utter dedication to wicketkeeping rubbed off on her:

> I really like working with Michael Bates. He's extremely passionate about wicketkeeping so when you work one on one with him, it's just refreshing. He's obviously extremely knowledgeable about wicketkeeping, but he comes to me with loads of new ideas every day. He'll bring that energy, which makes training interesting and fun. I'm really motivated to get better, maybe to the point of being a perfectionist, so we analyse everything and make loads of little technical tweaks throughout. I don't like not trying to get better, which I think should be a given. But when you're batting, sometimes you just go in, you have your net, and you leave. There are so many batters that I don't always get the technical attention that I love with my keeping. I like the granular detail. As a batter, you sometimes just go out and play on feel. With my keeping, it's different and I enjoy that challenge around it. I have deliberate things I say to myself and do with my stance in keeping, whereas I wouldn't do that batting.

It is quite obvious that the energy that Michael Bates brings to his wicketkeeping coaching has had a hugely positive impact on Amy, and we need to remember within this that she hasn't always loved wicketkeeping. There has been a huge transition for her.

> I wasn't always a keeper. In fact, it wasn't until I was nearly 16 and it was suggested to me when I went on

tour to South Africa with Warwickshire as we didn't have a back-up at the time. I actually have a really clear memory of one of my first games as a keeper. I didn't know what I was doing. I think I had some natural ability, but I didn't have any game awareness. I didn't know where to stand and the ball was bouncing twice before it got to me. I didn't have any confidence with it. You see, I've always loved batting and I've never been a reluctant batter, not ever. But I've been a reluctant keeper, yet I do love being a keeper now. Nowadays I see myself as a batter-keeper rather than a keeper-batter but only by maybe by a per cent. There's hardly anything in it now.

You can often learn so much about a cricketer when you ask them which cricketer they most admire. They will see in someone else what they want to see in themselves. And even if it is within you, it is just sometimes easier to describe it in someone else. This was the case when Amy and I talked about wicketkeepers she admired.

I really enjoy watching the Pakistan male wicketkeeper Mohammad Rizwan. He really stands out for me – I just love his energy. I was so impressed by him because he brings that intensity and energy to the game. I think I can have quite a languid kind of body language, similar to Jos Buttler, and it was actually good for me to watch Rizwan. I was literally sat there watching him and he made me feel like I wanted to go out and keep. It's funny because even though I would be more like Jos in the body language, I was more inspired by Rizwan, which is

similar to Batesy. They bring that energy and basically
it inspires me.

There it is again, that energy thing.

I found this theme fascinating because it dovetailed so
well with what other keepers have told me for this book but,
interestingly, in a slightly different way. Jack Russell described
the mental space he got himself into when keeping at his best
as the fiercest storm of intensity imaginable. It meant that at
that moment in time, he was incredibly invested in the game.
So much so that literally nothing else mattered in the world to
him at that precise moment. That might sound like hyperbole
to someone reading it for the first time but that is entirely
correct. In the heat of that moment, nothing else in the world
mattered to Jack Russell other than catching the ball. That
mental energy, intensity or passion was what made him one
of the greatest wicketkeepers of all time. Alec Stewart talked
about this but in a completely different way – it was almost
entirely focused on whether a wicketkeeper was prepared to
put the energy, intensity and dedication into the practice and
hard work required to be a top wicketkeeper. He admits turning
that mental switch on in 1996, and his keeping took off from
there. As I look back on the chapters so far, I can see that every
wicketkeeper in this book has talked about a level of energy
being required to be excellent at the role. And I agree – it does
mean that you are entirely invested in the game and, dare I say
it, more than anyone else on your team. As a wicketkeeper,
every ball while you are in the field is vitally important to you.
As a result, your memory of the game is photographic at times,
as Amy describes:

I think a top keeper could give a better debrief of a game than anyone else on the pitch or as good as anyone on the pitch. Sometimes I feel like I could tell you about every ball from an innings.

Ok, so you might now argue that keepers have a rest from the game while their team bats – that they are not super engaged then. Well, I would disagree. Yes, waiting to bat won't carry the same intensity as actual wicketkeeping but every keeper in this book has talked about how they are fascinated by the gritty detail of wicketkeeping and that they are constantly watching what other keepers are doing. So, as a starter, a keeper will be watching what the other keeper is doing during a batting innings. But it goes way beyond this. The whole game is of massive interest to a wicketkeeper because they have a role in all of it. They are the middle person in between the bowlers and the batters and who advises everyone, including the captain and coach. In truth, everyone wants the wicketkeeper's opinion. A top wicketkeeper is fully invested in the game in every way – they are ALL-IN. My chat with Amy really brought this to light for me because it was this particular theme that has inspired her to be a top international wicketkeeper. As I looked at this, I could see that it existed in the DNA of every good wicketkeeper and I could relate to this on a personal level as well. Throughout my career, I felt completely absorbed in matches. I wanted to be everything to everyone in the team because I felt like it was my role as the keeper. I felt like I had to be the heartbeat of every team that I was in, bringing the intensity and energy that we needed – trying to always be the drummer in the band. It was why I often felt completely exhausted at the end of a game.

It was only during and after my chat with Amy that I really started to see this connection between energy, intensity and passion being at the heart of what a true wicketkeeper is. Even as a keeper myself, I don't think I entirely appreciated this. And I think that this is enormously missed by people commentating about wicketkeepers within the media. In the vast majority of cases, they are looking at something physical (do they look like a keeper?) or something technical (do they move like a keeper?). When this is blended by a commentator's preconception of what they think a true wicketkeeper should look and move like then no wonder we get some fairly average analysis made. Those preconceptions are often borne from a wicketkeeper they have watched and admired in yesteryear. Although comments might not be said out loud exactly like this, the meaning behind many of them is that 'he or she doesn't look like a keeper to me'. The reality is that some keepers will be better than others, as with batters and bowlers, but I think a broader understanding of what makes a true wicketkeeper is missed a great deal in the chatter around the game.

This point aligns with what Alec Stewart said about the 'Keepers Union' – the name given to the community of wicketkeepers to which we all feel we belong:

> That's why I think that the 'Keepers Union' is a real thing. We all understand what we've been through, the tough times, what you have to put up with and the jobs you have to do. And that's why I think it is a unique club of people.

In simple terms, the Keepers Union exists because wicketkeepers often feel misunderstood by the wider cricketing community and therefore stick closely together. A couple of stories from Amy really enforced this for me:

> In the recent India series, Batesy and I had been playing around with my stance when standing up and I had only had a few sessions on it before the tour. I was standing slightly wider with a flat back to get my head and, therefore, weight further forward. During our early sessions, it felt really uncomfortable and I really wasn't sure. But pre-game, I was practising it with some underarms while wearing my cap and it felt great. It suddenly felt like it all clicked. But the thing is that when you have long hair, it's a nightmare. Well, actually, it's the long hair while wearing a helmet which is a nightmare. When I went down in my stance, the helmet just pushed down over my eyes and everything felt completely different. I was out there keeping for England and it felt horrible. I was so uncomfortable. And then I got a stumping that went up on the big screen and the girls rushed over and told me how quick and good I looked. As they were saying this and I was watching it on the big screen, I genuinely felt awful.

So, I then asked Amy if the opposite had happened – had there been occasions where she had received unwarranted criticism?

> There have been loads actually but one recently really stands out. Last summer in a T20 at Derby, I was standing up to a seamer and there was a massive nick. It hit me on the shoulder and my whole arm went numb

because it had hit the nerves on my shoulder. There was genuinely no way that I could have caught it because it was such a big edge. At the end of the innings, we went up to the changing rooms and the TV was on. I wasn't actually watching but someone told me that they were doing a little review of England's missed chances and that nick was on there. I was like, 'How can they call that?' It literally cannoned into my shoulder while I stood up. It was so annoying and frustrating. If I had dropped that while stood back, then fair enough, but I had no chance stood up, and there was no recognition of that.

Within those two stories, Amy pretty much summed up the life of the wicketkeeper. And these stories weren't while she was playing village cricket where a lack of knowledge might be understandable – this was while she was playing for England. If there can be this level of misunderstanding at the highest level of the game, then no wonder wicketkeepers get frustrated and stick with each other!

I asked Amy what you need to be a successful wicketkeeper.

In one word, I think you need to be strong. In your lower body, obviously, with strong legs. But also, in your core, so you can be strong positionally. You've got to be strong so you can move fast and just let your hands be free.

As Amy said all this about the physical attributes you might need to be a top keeper, I also thought about how the word 'strong' applied to so much about wicketkeeping. To be a player that engaged and invested in a game in which your skills are often misunderstood means that you really need to be strong mentally. You have to be prepared to be a one of a kind who will bring energy, intensity and leadership to a team throughout all of it. Ultimately, you have to be so in love with it that you'll put up with anything.

> I love being a keeper now. You're the only one in the team, which is funny because I've always hated attention. Actually, that's not strictly true because I've always enjoyed getting attention for how I play; I just don't like being the centre of attention in a social setting or team meeting or things like that. I just like that I'm good at something that's a bit unique. It's like my thing.

Amy was effectively a batter turned into a wicketkeeper. There was no immediate love affair or fascination with the art as there was for others. Indeed, she admits she was a reluctant keeper at times, but she told me as much about being a wicketkeeper as anyone in this book. Her connection with the energy of the role that has inspired her to be the best she can be spoke volumes.

I found this amazing quote from William Fiennes in an article he wrote called 'Taken: a love letter to the art of wicketkeeping':

> Baseball has a catcher, cricket has a keeper: you keep wicket, like a diary or a secret, the verb rich with suggestions of ownership and intimacy.

I love this quote and it relates to so much Amy and others have told me about wicketkeeping. Being a wicketkeeper is being in a different world to other cricketers. I think we feel a sense of pride and ownership about that. Deep down we know that most people won't truly understand what we do and how we do it, so we treasure those hidden secrets to what we do and discuss them amongst ourselves. But more than anything, we are all-in on being a wicketkeeper. We are fully invested in the role and the energy that we feel we need to bring to the game. It is what makes us tick. It is who we are on a cricket field. Ultimately, that might just be the true essence of a wicketkeeper.

AMY JONES CAREER AVERAGES

Batting & Fielding										
Format	Matches	Innings	Runs	HS	Ave	SR	100s	50s	Ct	St
WTEST	2	2	65	64	32.5	43.62	0	1	4	0
WODI	55	46	1186	94	27.58	82.47	0	9	36	9
WT20I	63	52	927	89	20.6	120.07	0	5	26	24

†Statistics as of 15/01/2022

Chapter 11

Peter Moores

I don't believe there is a man that I respect more in cricket than Peter Moores.

I'm not alone in thinking that, though – some of England's captains and finest players have spoken out about what an incredible man and coach Peter is. This level of respect often prompts an immediate question from supporters and media as to why this is so – 'What is so special about Peter?' The answer to this question is why I wanted to dedicate a chapter of this book to him; the fact that he was an outstanding wicketkeeper for Sussex and the England head coach twice are actually just bonuses to add on to this.

So, the answer as to why I and others think Peter is such a special cricket coach …

Peter is the purest cricket coach I have ever met. What I mean by this is that as a player working with him you are *never* in doubt that he is 100 per cent focused on making you better, whatever it takes and even if it is to his own detriment. He has no agenda other than making you better. This all might sound quite obvious and you might ask the question, 'Surely all cricket coaches are like this?' Well, in professional cricket particularly, this is rare. Lots of coaches carry agendas, just as many players do, and they are always borne from selfish reasons. People are often trying to enhance their careers and having the ear or voice of the right person at the right time can really help. For example, a coach giving preferential treatment to a high-profile player or ignoring a troublesome player are things that can easily happen. A coach blaming players when talking to the media, behind the scenes or out in the open can also happen. Those sorts of things don't even register with Peter – he is laser focused to make every player he works with better, regardless of sacrifice, internal politics or personal ambition.

I have a small example from my time at Lancashire with him. The development of white ball cricket was accelerating rapidly in the last few years of my career and the truth is that my game was struggling to keep up. If you were coming in at 7 or 8, as I was, then you needed to be able to score at more than 8 an over. That might not sound like much compared to today's standards, but ten or so years ago, it was a new standard. My place in the Lancashire white ball side was under some pressure but I was picked in the first game of the season at Old Trafford. I came in at 7 and struggled to score at much more than a run a ball – it wasn't good enough and I knew it. The game was on a Saturday and first thing on Sunday morning my phone starts ringing, and it is Peter: 'Hey Luke, listen, I think I know how we can really move forward your death hitting. Let's get in early tomorrow and get started with it.'

Again, this might not sound much but it really is. The easy option for the coach was to mentally take note that I wasn't good enough at that time to do the role I was being asked to do and needed to be dropped immediately or in the near future if things didn't improve. Instead, Peter, off his own bat, called me on a Sunday morning with a plan of how to make me better and was willing to give me more of his precious time to do so. Making me better might have even caused him a selection headache rather than taking the easy option of just dropping me, but that didn't matter to Peter – he just wanted to make me better. There were also so many other things he could have been focusing on that Sunday morning, including his own personal life, but he gave me time. And he was there, first thing on Monday morning, full of energy and enthusiasm as to how to help me improve. During our session I felt like he was completely focused on me, nothing else, but the reality was that he would have been thinking about a million different things to do with the squad. Yet he felt entirely present at our session. Every single player in the world would react brilliantly to that. That is just one small example from one player, but there are thousands of them with players all over the world. Anyone who works with Peter knows that all he cares about is making you better. Peter has many technical, tactical and motivational abilities as a coach but this particular part of him is what makes him incredibly special.

This is why I wanted Peter's take on what it truly means to be a wicketkeeper. He views the game so purely and honestly, and has such vast experience across it, that I knew he would produce many golden nuggets of insight in a short chat with him. I asked him what he thought about the role of the wicketkeeper in a team.

> I feel like you are there to serve a bit. You serve the team. From the warm-ups, to catching throws, taking a bowl, talking to bowlers about what they need, tidying up a bad throw, getting people going or whatever is required for the team. You're there to make people look good. Whatever it is, we'll tidy that up and get us back on track. That's why I also see keepers as part of the bowling

group because they're somebody you serve a lot. You are their partner in crime a little bit. So, you build that relationship with bowlers and when you've kept to them for a long time it becomes really strong, you get to know them really well. I think that ability of a keeper to work with bowlers is a huge tactical part of the game. I played in a televised final while at Sussex and took a stumping off Ian Salisbury. When the commentator, who I think was Christopher Martin-Jenkins, described the wicket, he referred to me as Ian's henchman. It was actually one of the biggest compliments he could give me because I was there to finish things off for people and help them work. That is being a keeper.

This answer said it all to me. Firstly, it perfectly summed Peter up as a person, coach and former wicketkeeper – he's there to serve and help people look good. But, secondly, this was also so true about wicketkeepers and an angle that no one else I had spoken to for this book had yet given. It prompted me to think about how a lot of long-term wicketkeepers in a team are generally very popular. Throughout my first-class cricket career, I can't remember many, if any, occasions when I heard a player describe the character of their incumbent wicketkeeper in anything but positive terms. Taking on Peter's point, I think that's because keepers are there to serve the team. They sit in the middle of the batsmen and the bowlers and are basically trying to help everyone. This might also be why, historically, we hold such affinity and romanticism for our legendary wicketkeepers – they are a favourite for many people.

So, I see wicketkeeping as totally a craft. I've seen a lot of people who can catch well but who don't become great keepers. There's a difference between being good in a drill and being good in a match. The great keepers that I've seen have the desire to constantly improve, because they see it as a craft, so they're driven by the desire to improve rather than by ego. It's the difference that it's not about 'Look at me'; it's more about, 'I just need to get better at that.' It's a Johnny Wilkinson kicking thing. To me, it's this desire to keep going that comes from somewhere deep.

Peter's words were perfect in pulling together what so many other people have said in this book. As an example, there was Alec Stewart's emphasis on someone having to be prepared to put the work in and Sarah Taylor's opinion that you are born to be a keeper – two different ends of the spectrum of what makes a great keeper. Yet both points were summed up perfectly by Peter. You do need that desire to put the work in but for the great keepers this desire comes from somewhere deep; maybe they are even born with it – the desire to master their craft.

It reminded me of a book I had recently read by Daniel Pink called *Drive: The Surprising Truth About What Motivates Us*. Pink discusses in depth the difference between intrinsic and extrinsic motivation: intrinsic motivation comes from a deep place of purpose, mastery and ownership, versus extrinsic motivation coming from the potential external rewards such as money and fame. Pink's overall point is that extrinsic motivation is far more powerful than intrinsic motivation in so many ways. All of this fell into place for me on the point that Peter was making about great wicketkeepers – they are absolutely driven by intrinsic motivation. Becoming a master craftsman is not about the big 'I am', it is something borne from a very different place. Within this discussion, the question could be asked as to whether it is still possible to produce a great wicketkeeper who is only driven by the fame and money that would come from it. Well, in trying to answer that, let's consider the actual role again.

Wicketkeeping is a lonely job. Few people in the game, let alone your team, truly understand what you do. You can be criticised for things you shouldn't be and feel your best work is often underappreciated. Everyone has an opinion on what you're doing and they often give it whether you have asked for it or not. You're there to serve the team and sit between batters and bowlers within team dynamics. You are the only player on the field aiming to be perfect every single day of your career but are left to self-mark yourself more often than not. And, finally, it is physically very painful at times. So, if you want to do this and be brilliant at it then you bloody well need to be obsessed with it on a deep level! If you're motivated by external recognition or money, then you are likely to find other ways to get this rather than by being a wicketkeeper. I guess that I have always known this somewhere in my subconscious, but the way Peter explained it made it crystal clear as to what being a true wicketkeeper is really all about:

> You've got to have a standard. You've got to have an inbuilt standard of what you are as a keeper. Trying to achieve perfection is an inbuilt standard that you have and won't let go of. It's why I used to hate to keep in a

benefit game or any game that didn't have anything on it, because I knew I couldn't find my standard.

The more I talked to Peter, the more I could see how the great keepers have something very unique internally. They are being driven by a standard that they are setting themselves in what at times can seem like a fairly thankless task, and they are completely obsessed about it! I would take you back to how Jack Russell talked about wicketkeeping. He described the fiercest of the intensities within him that would take him to a place of absolute clarity about what he was trying to do – it was him or the ball, and he was not going to lose. Without exaggeration, nothing else mattered in the world to him at that moment in time. When you take all this into account, it is no wonder that wicketkeeping has attracted some more than quirky characters over the history of the game. The battles or processes going on within a wicketkeeper might well be greater than in a player in any other position on the field.

So, why are there fewer quirky characters wicketkeeping in top-level cricket nowadays?

Well, my take would be there are fewer quirky players full stop. If you go to old footage of all international players, there was much more variation in styles than there is now. I just think that now people watch everybody else and they can see everything that people are doing and copy them really well. So, there are styles that get copied. I still think there are characters in the modern game, but maybe in slightly different ways. The modern player is slightly different in how they go about things. They're pretty diverse still, they're not all the same, but they can quickly see a thread of how something works because they are watching each other so much.

Again, to bring this back to Jack Russell: he said that his main source of wicketkeeping advice and information when he was a young wicketkeeper was when he played Derbyshire with Bob Taylor and Kent with Alan Knott twice a year. He couldn't wait for those games so he could study and talk to them. He was basically starved of information on how he could improve his absolute obsession in life; and yet, the modern wicketkeeper just needs to click a button to do this now. So, in previous generations of wicketkeepers, they were often trying to work it out for themselves and when they found a method that worked for them, whether standing up or standing back, they would then obsess over it in a bid for perfection. It reminded me of watching Karl Krikken keep wicket at Derbyshire with an entirely unique style. It was a method that he had just worked out for himself. With odd movements, constant twitches and a gorillalike stance, it looked strange, but he was bloody brilliant. To develop that style pretty much on your own, to a level that you can repeat again and again at the highest level, then you are likely to be quite a quirky character. Karl was certainly that!

Peter tells a similar tale about how he got wicketkeeping information when he was younger:

The thing I remember growing up with, which I've still got actually, is Alan Knott's book on wicketkeeping. I think it's got a picture of him on the front with those red gloves. That became like the Bible to me. Knotty was the first one that influenced me in a big way, but Bob Taylor was a bit of a hero for me. And Bob was not a huge quirky character. I got to play against him very early in my career and I remember asking him if he could watch me keep, which he did and came to me after and gave me some great advice. It was the efficiency of Bob's wicketkeeping that I loved. It was like he never moved. I used to really enjoy playing against Bruce French on the circuit as well. I enjoyed him as a keeper but also his company. I really looked forward to playing and we would talk a lot about wicketkeeping.

It was interesting that Peter mentioned 'efficiency' as it was something both Chris Read and Geraint Jones talked about. There's a definite thread in that many keepers are searching for efficiency and rhythm. I look back on my career and can identify with this. The search for efficiency is crucial because this is a skill you are repeating hundreds a time each day. Imagine trying to be a wicketkeeper with an inefficient and difficult technique – it would actually be tortuous. And rhythm flows alongside efficiency. I used to watch James Foster keep wicket with such envy as he produced extraordinary bits of skill while seemingly in perfect rhythm – like he was born to do it. This rhythm has important practicalities though. As a wicketkeeper you are expending an enormous amount of energy each day and if you're not able to find a rhythm to that then you will quickly become exhausted. With exhaustion comes inconsistency.

I still think it takes a couple of seasons before you start to find the rhythm of keeping. And I think that until you find the rhythm to your style of keeping, it's very difficult to be really consistent. You might keep really well once, but it's about doing it again and again. That rhythm is in all great keepers.

Once you really pinpoint efficiency and rhythm as being key elements of being a top keeper then you can absolutely see how wicketkeeping is a true craft of the game. And as with all crafts, it takes time to master it. With a musician or a painter, there will be the odd very young genius who comes along, but most will need time to mature before they truly master their discipline. This also seems to answer the question as to why keepers are often so obsessed by their kit, whether it is their gloves or the position of their collars, or anything else for that matter. Craftsmen always take great care with their tools and that is no different for keepers. Peter even talks about it being a big reason why he started wicketkeeping:

> If I'm honest, I probably started wicketkeeping because I liked the kit. We're going back to the day with kitbags with just a couple bats, gloves and pads. I liked the thought of getting all the kit and putting it all on. So, I think that's probably where it started.

Like a true master, Peter painted a beautifully clear picture for me of what being a wicketkeeper really was all about – maybe better than anyone else. Wicketkeeping really is a craft and it requires absolute dedication if you want to master it. It's not a glamour role and therefore requires particular characters to keep persisting with it. What really became clear to me after my chat with Peter was that despite the role of the wicketkeeper feeling like it has changed so much, the fundamentals of what wicketkeeping really is are still very much alive and kicking.

> I think the modern keeper is pulled around quite a bit. There are three different formats. They're expected to bat well in all formats and keeping has to go along with it. The challenges on the modern keeper are high, really high, and that needs some quality work to go into it. In fact, I think that keepers have to nearly get burned first before they truly get it. I think of Matt Prior when he went into the England team – he kept pretty well but made some mistakes. It meant he had to go away and then really do what I would say was the volume of work required to understand his own game. Then he could go back to that level and deliver consistently under real pressure. Before that, he was just a really talented keeper but not to the level of understanding his own rhythm.

What Peter is describing so brilliantly is mastery. Matt Prior went through a process that I think almost all top keepers go through in order to begin to master their craft. It reminded me of watching James Foster performing for England as a young wicketkeeper versus watching an absolute master in action when keeping for Essex towards the end of his career. As Jack Russell has also pointed out, he dropped two catches on his Test debut, one of which was very straightforward, yet went on to become one of the greatest wicketkeepers of all time.

My chat with Peter crystallised so much for me about wicketkeeping. We never talked about what a wicketkeeper should sound and look like, but instead, what the role truly required and the characteristics you needed in order to master it.

To be a great wicketkeeper, you need to be a master craftsman.

PETER MOORES CAREER AVERAGES

| Batting & Fielding | | | | | | | | | | | |
Format	Matches	Innings	Runs	HS	Ave	SR	100s	50s	Ct	St
FC	231	345	43	7351	185	24.34		7	31	502	44
List A	245	193	46	2603	89*	17.7		0	8	225	32

Chapter 12

Michael Bates

I didn't originally plan on speaking to Michael Bates for this book, but he came up so strongly in my conversations with Jos Buttler, Sarah Taylor and Amy Jones that I really wanted him to be part of it. It wasn't actually how much those three brought his name up, it was more the context in which they did – they talked about him as being a 'true wicketkeeper' as a player, and now, as a coach. Investigating that label was really what this whole book was about. What was it about Michael that made him so pure in that role versus others? The fact that Michael was now working as a coach at the top level meant that his insight was going to be invaluable.

I played against Michael a little bit towards the back end of my career but watched him a lot, as I did every wicketkeeper. He was an exceptional gloveman and his work on the last ball of Hampshire's CB40 final win versus Warwickshire in 2012 was a great illustration of that. Neil Carter was leading a charge to win the game for the Bears and they only needed one off the final ball. Michael was stood up to the stumps as Kabir Ali bowled the final ball. In an attempt to bowl a yorker, Ali bowled a fast, low, full toss just outside the off stump. Carter swung and missed, and Michael took the ball perfectly to win the game. The take itself very much reminded me of Geraint Jones's take off Kabir Ali, again for England to win a One Day International against South Africa off the last ball of the match. They were both examples of exceptional wicketkeeping. To the untrained eye, they might have seemed fairly straightforward because both wicketkeepers looked so still when they took the ball; however, within that simplicity was technique, mindset and nerve of the highest order. The ability to make something look so simple when there's so much distraction and pressure in play is what top wicketkeepers can do.

> Being honest – and I don't want to sound bad – it didn't even cross my mind that I would mess it up. Literally. I was thinking of nothing. I just knew that if I did what I'd done for every single ball previously, I'd nail it. I just knew. And I knew without knowing, without consciously knowing.

Michael is describing that beautiful place where a wicketkeeper can get to of ultimate 'flow'. It is almost like he or she is in autopilot mode and just delivering the skill that they were born to do. However, some wicketkeepers find this more consistently and easier than others. I felt like I often battled to find it, but for Michael it was different.

> That natural flow state that I was able to slide into as a keeper used to just happen almost always. I put the gloves on, I've crossed the line and that was it – I'd be able to do brilliant things without thinking too much about it. My batting was on the opposite end of that scale so I could always notice the massive difference in the two.

There was definitely something about how Michael talked about wicketkeeping that was very pure. He was able to deliver his skill at an elite level without too much stress or thought – it was very natural. As I write this, it takes me back to Sarah Taylor's view that you are born to be a wicketkeeper. It definitely sounded like Michael was born to do this on a skill base level.

> Wicketkeeping is 100 per cent a craft. Yeah, absolutely it is. I think you can manufacture it, but it will never quite be as good as if you just naturally have it. As I said, if you're a decent catcher, you can build someone up to be pretty good, but they're never going to be as good as a Jack Russell.

The question that screamed out for me from this was what was '*if you just naturally have it*' – what was the '*it*'? Is this a skill-based thing? Michael clearly had an immense amount of natural ability as a wicketkeeper but is that what he was referring to?

> You are literally the heart and soul of the team – that is it. I think it's so important for keepers to appreciate that, to always want to try and influence the game, to understand that they're not a passenger in the game that just collects the ball. They're there to affect the game.

It was becoming clear that Michael was talking about a mindset thing rather than anything skill based.

> It's a fundamental belief of mine that keepers like Jack Russell and James Foster have the innate ability to

anticipate the ball coming to them: every time the batter misses it or nicks it, it's as if they knew it was going to happen … to the point where it looks like they're one step ahead of everyone else. MS Dhoni is one of the best examples of this stood up; it's like he knows in advance that the batter is going to miss it. I think this element of wicketkeeping is very difficult to teach but is part of the mindset required. I would add to this, I often wonder whether the less 'pure' keepers, the batters who keep, struggle more with this as they naturally adopt more of a batter's mindset when keeping, in that they almost do the opposite and expect the batter to hit the ball. For example, they see a half volley and simply switch off, expecting the batter to hit it. Inevitably this mentality stands to cause all sorts of problems.

Up to this point in the book, I feel like we have skirted around the topic of 'thinking like a keeper'. We have talked about it generally but maybe not as directly as Michael has in this section. The question as to how and why someone thinks like a true wicketkeeper is an interesting one. Maybe you are born like that or maybe it is just because you are entirely invested in the craft. For example, you may have lived the life of a wicketkeeper for so long and dedicated so much towards it that your brain is entirely wired to think like one. Alec Stewart is a decent reference of a wicketkeeper who became an excellent one but turned that switch on much later in his cricketing life than many others. However, when the switch was flicked, he utterly dedicated himself to the art. Michael's view on this was:

I think that to be a proper keeper, you've got to want to do it, because without that, you aren't able to capture what I've just said about being the heart and soul of the team. You won't be able to appreciate why you're there. You won't be able to capture that desire to want the ball and to affect the game positively. If you're passive and you don't really want to be there, or you're doing it because it's getting you in the team, then I think you've lost straight away. You've lost the battle. And actually, as a coach now, if someone is a good catcher and they want to do it – that's all I need to know. You can work with that. They can catch a ball half decently and they've got a drive to do it and they want to do it, then I'm giving them the gloves every day of the week.

The theme of 'desire' came through so strongly in my chats with Alec Stewart, Jack Russell, Peter Moores, Jos Buttler and now, with Michael. In truth, I probably expected this from guys like Alec or Jos, who, by their own admission, had to work incredibly hard to establish their careers as wicketkeepers. But I found it fascinating that this also came from the likes of Jack and Michael – the keepers whom some would describe as natural wicketkeepers. It looked like it came to them so easily and even Michael described the flow of wicketkeeping as something he found quite naturally. Yet, despite this, 'desire' came through from Michael and Jack as the strongest requisite to be a top keeper.

I have asked everyone in this book who their wicketkeeping heroes were. This was partly out of interest but also because I believe you can tell a lot about someone in who they particularly admire. We often find it easier to highlight the characteristics and skills we desire or love in ourselves when we see them in someone else. Amy Jones was interesting in this respect because she picked out Mohammad Rizwan as the keeper that she most admired. She said it was his energy and enthusiasm that she loved. Watching him keep wicket made her want to go and do it herself. It was Rizwan's energy that Amy felt she sometimes lacked and wanted to bring to the game. I found Michael's answer to this equally fascinating:

> Alec Stewart. I always remember watching him, desperately wanting a pair of his gloves. I don't know if you remember them, they were great. I desperately wanted a pair of them, but never did. But yeah, I used to try and emulate him quite a bit like with his collar up. In the Hampshire kit when I was a kid, we were only ever given three-quarter length shirts so I used to make my parents buy me long sleeves so I could look like Alec. He was very chirpy, bubbly and just very outwardly energetic as a keeper, and I wonder whether on some level that rubbed off on me too. It was something that I brought very naturally to my keeping as well. And I love that. I love the fact that he wasn't the most naturally gifted, fluent keeper, but still got himself to such a brilliant level. I admire people who just work their nuts off. I have so much respect for that. So, I absolutely loved that about Alec.

In a book that has so heavily debated the merits of what people perceive as 'true wicketkeepers', I found it so interesting that a pure wicketkeeper like Michael would pick out a more manufactured wicketkeeper as his hero. It just really reinforced the point that Michael was making about mindset being the real driver of what made a top wicketkeeper. For all the natural ability he was able to show and saw in others, he would keep coming back to this mindset:

> I think it's difficult to be a very good keeper if you've got a bit of an ego – it's a selfless job. We absolutely love giving to people. We love seeing someone else succeed and go out there and nail it. I think that's our drive, isn't it? Bringing everyone with you, being the energy giver, being in the centre of everything, just leading and driving everything forward – I think that's our motivation. That's what we get the kick out of and that's not necessarily recognised particularly.

This aligned so perfectly with what Peter Moores said of wicketkeepers – they are there to serve the team. Wicketkeepers, by nature, require a mindset that sees them as a leader in the team, but crucially, one that holds the team's and their teammates' success above theirs rather than one that drags the team forward through their individual successes. Top wicketkeepers undoubtedly cherish their personal successes but there is something deeper within them that makes them want their successes to be put forward to the service of helping the whole team. Michael's comments on this are illuminating:

> I think that's something that Jos Buttler has in spades. The impression I get is that he is an exceptional leader and whether he's performing or not would be the first

name on the team sheet for that particular reason. So, I think he's a brilliant example of how that is still so true. And I'd use Amy Jones as an example as well – I've seen her grow so much over the last couple of years, and she's evolving. She's becoming so much more confident and she's becoming a genuine leader in her own way and a better wicketkeeper as a result.

Michael was one of the last wicketkeepers I spoke to for this book, but I felt that during my chat with him we were finally getting very close to what it truly means to be a wicketkeeper. It wasn't just his views that made me feel this way but also his own personal experience in trying to make his way to the top of the game as what some people would describe as a 'pure wicketkeeper'. What I mean by that is that Michael was seen as an outstanding gloveman who needed his batting to keep pace if he was going to survive – more of a Jack Russell than an Alec Stewart.

> The sad thing is, and this is what I've kind of realised since writing my own book and reflecting on my own career, is I massively undervalued my contribution to the team. I think because of all the hype around the importance of batting, I was very aware of the pressure I felt to get more runs and to contribute with the bat more. And that is genuinely how I valued myself – my contribution to the team is whether I batted well. I almost disregarded what I was doing with the gloves, which is so sad. And it's one of my biggest regrets – I didn't just embrace what I was able to do, I didn't embrace my talent, I didn't appreciate

it enough and I didn't appreciate quite the impact that I was having on our team, especially our one-day team.

The perception and role of the wicketkeeper in world cricket went through the biggest change when Adam Gilchrist played, basically because everyone wanted one of him. However, I think there was another evolution of wicketkeepers during the back end of my career and the start of Michael's. As I described in my chapter with Peter Moores, it was acceptable to be able to score at 7 or 8 an over at the death of a one-day game in my last year or so of professional cricket. Wicketkeepers batting at 7, 8 or 9 would often be batting in those final overs. Yet, from 2012 to today, scoring at 7 or 8 an over is not good enough. Teams are looking for people to be able to score at 10-plus an over in this period of the game. The pressure on wicketkeepers to be able to 'strike' has never been greater. Michael's career sat right in the middle of this evolution and his own words tell you how much it affected him. He was an exceptional wicketkeeper who made match-winning contributions with the gloves in one-day cricket, yet even he started to see that as of secondary importance. Yet, imagine if he hadn't taken that last ball off Kabir Ali in the 2012 CB40 final so perfectly … Hampshire wouldn't have won the trophy.

Even before I got my first professional contract, that was always the case; I would always have to work super hard on my batting. I always needed to score more runs and I just couldn't escape it. And I think people built up this perception of me being this exceptional keeper but wasn't good enough for the bat. And I don't think I was ever ultimately able to shift that perception. I probably put more pressure on myself and made it a bigger thing than perhaps it was, but it was constant. I was just always so aware of it.

There is no debate over whether wicketkeepers need to bat well in today's game; they simply do, in exactly the same way that all bowlers, unless truly exceptional, need to offer something with the bat. But the fascinating part of Michael's experience is that within all this, the value of his wicketkeeping was lost somewhere and to no one more than to himself. Just maybe within that loss, he forgot the true essence of what he was about as a cricketer … indeed, as a wicketkeeper.

> I genuinely think that all that I experienced as a player has shaped how I am as a coach to wicketkeepers. I'm always so keen to reiterate how important a role they play and encourage them never to downplay the contribution that they make and to treasure that – to be there to make a difference.

In my opinion, Michael has shaped his style as a coach through his experiences as a player. He will always work to remind wicketkeepers what their true essence is and that they are vitally important givers to the team. Their energy, desire and attitude are what hold a team together during the toughest of moments. Indeed, it is exactly those qualities that Sarah Taylor and Amy Jones both mentioned that Michael brought to his coaching. There is only one wicketkeeper, and that screams of importance

– they need to be a leader within that group that is prepared to watch others look brilliant while they tidy up behind them. They are prepared to appear invisible and be misunderstood while others take the limelight. If a wicketkeeper forgets all this then they have begun to lose what they are truly about within the game.

Despite Michael being the wicketkeeper with the lowest profile that I interviewed for this book, I felt like his insight might just have been the most rounded. In many ways he had been an old-school wicketkeeper trying to make his way in a rapidly modernising game and had now transitioned into a coach to try to help the next generation of keepers. This gave him an amazing view on where wicketkeeping had come from and where it was heading. I was interested to know why he thought there were fewer quirky characters as wicketkeepers nowadays. He didn't necessarily have the answer for this, but he did make a fascinating observation about how body shapes have changed over the years:

> I think the look of a keeper has changed a lot. I actually don't think there's any doubt about that. When you look at keepers throughout the world, I think they look different because of what they now need to do with the bat. I think again of Jos Butter as an example – he's pretty tall, strong, solid, powerful, and he's able to whack the ball out of the park of fun. And that is how a lot of keepers now approach their batting. I think that's why keepers look different now. Keepers of old, like Jack Russell and me to an extent, the kind of smaller, scratchier keepers, don't exist much anymore. James Foster probably still

falls into that old-school bracket. He's tall, yeah, but he's quite slight. And he's got success from getting up and under the ball when batting – sweeping, reversing and being inventive, as opposed to that kind of big, strong, dominating whack-the-ball-out-of-the-ground sort of keeper.

I think this is an excellent point from Michael. Of course, not at all wicketkeepers are shaped for power hitting but the vast majority of them are nowadays. I guess this leads nicely into the question of whether all these changes in the role and shape of wicketkeepers have affected the quality of wicketkeeping in today's game. I think there are some old romantics who want to believe that no one will ever be as good as Alan Knott, Bob Taylor and Jack Russell, but I don't think that's true. International and domestic cricket still see some truly exceptional glovework today. Ben Foakes is an example that immediately springs to mind – a tall wicketkeeper, who has a similar shape to James Foster but with more power and yet is as good a wicketkeeper as there is in the world today. The standard of Foakes's wicketkeeping would rival most wicketkeepers of yesteryear.

It's an interesting question. I think of taller keepers like Quinton de Kock and Jos, and I think they're very good stood back because they rely on their athleticism. They rely on their power. They treat it like goalkeeping. They know that if they're in a good position and they're kind of on it they can rely on their natural ability to dive, to move, to catch and do a decent job of it. But stood up for me is the real art. That's the point of difference. And now you're asking the question, I wonder if quality has been lost from standing up – maybe there has. I wonder whether those physical attributes that allow these players to whack the ball out of the ground and allows them to be super athletic might just hold them back slightly when stood up.

Both Michael and I would agree there isn't a simple answer to this debate other than to say that in a game that has pulled hard on the role of the wicketkeeper, there still exist examples of exceptional glovework everywhere.

As I look back on my chat with Michael, the most powerful part of our conversation was how he was able to pinpoint what it really meant to be a true wicketkeeper. It wasn't about style, shape or technique, it was all about the mindset you brought to the beautiful craft of wicketkeeping. It was all about how a wicketkeeper could identify with what they brought to the team and why that was so vitally important – their energy, their desire and, most importantly, their willingness to place the team's needs in front of theirs. I felt a little sad that Michael lost sight of this while he was playing and the enormous contributions that he brought to the Hampshire side he played in, but equally happy that he could now reflect on that and make sure it was a key element to his coaching style.

I came away from our chat feeling clearer about where this book was taking me but also very glad that Michael is a top-level wicketkeeping coach now. Our young keepers are in safe hands with him.

MICHAEL BATES CAREER AVERAGES

| Batting & Fielding | | | | | | | | | | |
Format	Matches	Innings	Runs	HS	Ave	SR	100s	50s	Ct	St
FC	52	69	1177	103	19.94	45.19	1	5	149	7
List A	39	18	111	24*	10.09	68.94	0	0	25	4
T20	39	10	63	15	10.5	98.43	0	0	18	10

Chapter 13

Keith Piper

K eith Piper's wicketkeeping was mentioned in glowing terms by every single wicketkeeper I spoke to for this book. Considering the calibre of keepers I have consulted, that is quite something.

I was lucky enough to play against Keith once or twice towards the end of his career and his keeping really was breathtaking at times. He had this look of casual arrogance about his wicketkeeping, as if he was trying to show everyone how ridiculously easy he found the difficult art. With relaxed arms and straightish legs, he would catch the ball as if it was barely a bother to him – like the most natural thing he could ever do in his life. His style and brilliance created this aura around his wicketkeeping. Indeed, he felt intimidating behind the stumps as if he was playing the game on a level that most of us could never reach. Whether he was standing back to the lightning pace of Alan Donald or standing up to medium pacers or spinners, Keith's wicketkeeping was exceptional. He may not have played any senior international cricket but there is no question that his wicketkeeping was world class.

In 2020, Keith was voted the greatest ever Warwickshire CCC wicketkeeper by the club's supporters. With 44 per cent of the vote, he saw off the likes of Dick Lilley, Tiger Smith, Dick Spooner, Geoff Humpage and Tim Ambrose. This award recognised his wicketkeeping brilliance but also the significant influence he had on the Bears' huge success in the mid-1990s. That team was captained by Dermot Reeve, and this is what he said about him:

> Keith was a phenomenal wicketkeeper but much more than that. He would spot things and come up to me and say: 'Captain, Glads hasn't got his hand behind the ball like he does normally,' and I'd have a word with Gladstone, and he'd nod and put it right again. The number of little things Keith said that helped ... he was a very influential guy.

I really chased Keith down to be part of this book. My gut feeling told me that someone with that extraordinary natural brilliance behind the stumps must truly know what the essence of being a wicketkeeper is all about. From afar it looked like wicketkeeping flowed through his veins. This is what he had to say:

> There was a club called Tottenham Youth Club that I went to as a kid and they played cricket – it was Tottenham Cricket Club. I just bowled and battled or tried to, but I wasn't very good. It was more that I was around people and getting out of the house, really, to be honest. And then one day there was no one wicketkeeping, so I said I'd do it just to get involved. And I'll never ever forget this. There was a ball that was bowled down the leg side, and I don't know how I did it, but I just moved my legs down the leg side, took this ball beautifully into my hands. And from that day, I knew I loved catching a cricket ball because it just felt so natural. I fell in love

with it. Straight away, the ball melting into my hands, it just felt right. I can still see it now. Talking about it, I can see myself moving down the leg side, taking this one ball and the way it felt in my hands, it just melted into my gloves. It just felt like love.

'It just felt like love' – a short but incredibly powerful sentence from Keith. As soon as he started to speak about wicketkeeping, it was crystal clear that this was never 'just a job' for him. From the very first ball he caught, he found a home. From that very moment, wicketkeeping felt like a true purpose in his life. It was a place where he felt like he truly belonged.

What did wicketkeeping mean to me? I had to be the conductor of the orchestra on the field. I believed I had to dictate the tempo of the game. I influenced field placing, angles, all that kind of stuff; but I was mainly the energy in the field. And I think everybody got their energy off me. I was the Conductor of the Energy if you like!

I found it fascinating again that a wicketkeeper with such natural ability immediately lent towards the importance of an attribute like energy rather than, for instance, catching. You see, wicketkeeping has a tangible measure of success: catch the ball equals good; drop the ball equals bad. Yet almost every wicketkeeper in this book has described their role using something that is not tangible, like energy or attitude or mindset. As a comparison, I don't know of a batsman or bowler who measures their primary importance to the team via anything else other than runs or wickets. Jimmy Anderson is England's greatest ever bowler because he takes more wickets than anyone else … that's the top and bottom of it. Yet, with wicketkeeping there seems to be more to it.

> The difference between good and great wicketkeepers is the mindset. I think we could all have the talent but if we haven't got the mindset, I don't think we can achieve greatness. I did things with a positive mindset, which others tried with a negative mindset, and it didn't quite work. It was all mindset. Don't get me wrong, I might get a little worried about messing up because we're on telly or it's an important semi-final or final, but as soon as we crossed that white line, my positive side came into play, and it was like, 'I'm going to show everybody out here how good I am.' The interesting thing is, when I batted, I couldn't get into that mindset. My brain was all over the place when I batted. But keeping I could control my mind and my body in terms of I didn't really think of much apart from triggers like, 'He's going to nick this ball.' Sometimes I would just tell myself that I'm going to show the crowd how much energy I've got. It was almost like sometimes I could see when we were going down in the field and that's when I would like to switch it up and become more energised.

There they are again – those intangible qualities that might just be required to be a truly great wicketkeeper. It was also interesting to hear Keith refer to one of his wicketkeeping mental triggers as 'He's going to nick this ball.' That very much aligns with the point that keepers like Keith, Jack Russell, James Foster and MS Dhoni 'think' like wicketkeepers and are almost always able to anticipate what's about to happen.

> I believe your mindset should be that you want to make a difference in the game. That was mine. When I first joined Warwickshire, and I will never forget this, we were practising on the Colts Ground at Edgbaston. It was my first year at the club and probably my second or third session at that time. I was 18 years old, and Dermot Reeve was vice-captain at the time. I was keeping wicket during a middle practice and Dermot was walking across the car park to come and practise with us. He was always late, by the way. Someone bowled a really wide ball down the leg side. I flew horizontal and took this ball one-handed. And I will never forget Dermot shout, 'Bloody hell! This guy is a genius!' For me it was like, if the vice-captain of the club is saying that then I must be decent. From that moment on, I just wanted to show how good I was, I wanted to make a difference in the first team.

The way that Keith describes all this is so telling for me. He doesn't talk about it in a sense that he needs 'to do his job' and just catch balls. He's talking about wicketkeeping as having a bigger purpose within the game – a role in the match that can hugely influence others and make a real difference. Keith is describing the same thing that Michael Bates described as having lost when he played – the true essence of what a wicketkeeper brings to a team. As Bates described in his chapter, he was so consumed by what his batting could or couldn't do that he lost sight of what his wicketkeeping was bringing to that successful Hampshire one-day side. Wicketkeeping was so natural for him that he took it for granted while focusing on the 'struggle' of batting. It feels to me like Keith has never lost this understanding of what a truly great wicketkeeper can bring to the team.

It was difficult to imagine that someone as gifted as Keith ever looked on at other wicketkeepers with any envy over how good they were, but there were two.

Jack Russell epitomises wicketkeeping – everything he did, the way he took the ball, just the way he looked. For me, everything about him was how a keeper should look. I've seen him take stumpings where the ball has nipped back through the gate while he's standing up. The batsman jumped in the air because it's cut them in half and Jack took the ball over middle and leg, standing up, and took the bails off while the guy was still in the air. Unreal. So, Jack Russell, for me, is the number one ever in the history of the game. 100 per cent. And when I first started at Surrey, there was a guy in the second team called Graham Brown. He was shorter than me but was phenomenal. He couldn't bat but he would have got through just on his keeping. He would have played for England, in my opinion. So yeah, Jack Russell and Graham Brown.

What was clear in talking to Keith was that he has an enormous connection to the art of wicketkeeping – he feels it, he understands it, wicketkeeping is very much part of who he is. It was completely natural for him.

When I was keeping at my best, I didn't really feel anything. When I started thinking about stuff, that's when my body would get tenser. So, it was more about not thinking or feeling. It was more about just doing. My subconscious came into play a lot more because I'm sure, you know, the subconscious wants to do, whereas the conscious is a rationaliser – he's going to bowl short, he's going to bowl this one down the leg side, he's going to do things we can't affect. So, I just relaxed, watched the ball, and then reacted to it. It was the same with practising, to be honest. When we were practising, I didn't do much wicketkeeping. I caught a few balls. But that was it because when I started to think too much, my body started to tense up and, as you know, relaxed muscles work better than tense. So, I just let it happen. But don't get me wrong – you have your triggers, like 'He's going to nick this,' and 'Watch the ball.'

There was nothing manufactured about Keith's wicketkeeping – whether in his technique or his mind. He truly was a wicketkeeper in natural ability and persona, and what I find really interesting is that he doesn't ever mention one particular thing – technique. In fact, technique is barely mentioned throughout this book by any of the wicketkeepers, yet it is often the first thing looked at when a wicketkeeper is receiving a critique from the media. That, just in itself, shows you why there is such a huge gap in understanding what wicketkeeping and wicketkeepers are truly about. Technical analysis certainly has a role and I have recently watched an excellent explanation on television from

Matt Prior on why Jos Buttler's balance and body position meant he dropped a catch in the second Ashes Test match. However, I wonder if that is because we often see technique as an easy avenue to explain something to someone who doesn't understand it – it provides a tangible explanation. Yet it can't be any coincidence that 95 per cent of this book, which is being told by some of the best wicketkeepers we have ever produced, doesn't mention it. Instead, the focus has been on intangible attributes around mindset and desire that people will find much harder to understand. If you have a two- or three-minute window to explain why someone has dropped a catch, then it will be much easier to talk about a technicality rather than what might be going on inside that wicketkeeper's head.

I would like to add to the point above that this doesn't also mean that wicketkeepers should not be taught the correct techniques and that they shouldn't be drilled into them. Of course they should. The point is that there is a vast array of skills and attributes outside of technique that wicketkeepers need to live and breathe in order to deliver those very techniques. That is why the keepers in this book have talked about things like energy, attitude and focus before mentioning hand positions or body weight. I think the representation of wicketkeeping within the media gets this the wrong way round a lot of the time and therefore so does the true understanding of what being a wicketkeeper is all about.

During my conversations with certain wicketkeepers for this book, I could see that their connection with wicketkeeping was something quite profound. That connection perhaps separated them from others onto another level. I would put Jack Russell in that category and include the likes of Keith Piper and

Sarah Taylor. It felt like they all had found their home with wicketkeeping. They respected and embodied everything they believed represented being a wicketkeeper – it was truly who they were. There was absolutely nothing about their wicketkeeping that was manufactured – the energy, mindset, attitude, and skill – they all came naturally to them. Keith's thoughts on this were:

> I think you can make someone who wants to be a keeper into an adequate wicketkeeper, someone that does the job but doesn't bring any more to the table. But I think your greats and your best wicketkeepers are born with the skill and the mindset. I believe that someone who's made into a wicketkeeper is always just surviving, whereas with a great or natural wicketkeeper then they are always thriving and making a difference to the game.

As Keith said this, I identified with it a great deal. I was a professional wicketkeeper for fifteen or so years but for long periods of that time I did feel like I was just surviving. I was fighting to just be good enough to be at the top. It might sound crazy to someone looking in on my career, but that's true. I'm not sure I ever entirely relaxed into being a wicketkeeper, which is very different to the language that Keith used to describe his wicketkeeping. From the age of 18, when Dermot Reeve shouted across the Warwickshire CCC practice ground at Edgbaston that he was a genius, Keith knew deep within him that he was a true wicketkeeper. He knew he was blessed to do something that could make a difference to a team he played in.

Keith was the last wicketkeeper that I spoke to for this book, and I was glad about that. He was different to everyone else whilst carrying some similarities with the likes of Jack Russell and Sarah Taylor. There was a relaxed flow to the way he spoke about it that is perhaps reflected in how he kept wicket – natural, supremely confident, and almost like it was easy for him.

In my opinion, Keith was a great wicketkeeper and I believe he knows that too. I think that is why he could so eloquently separate the difference between good and great.

There will not be many wicketkeepers like Keith Piper in the beautiful game of cricket.

KEITH PIPER CAREER AVERAGES

| Batting & Fielding | | | | | | | | | | |
Format	Matches	Innings	Runs	HS	Ave	SR	100s	50s	Ct	St
FC	200	275	4618	116*	19.99	–	2	14	504	36
List A	237	127	970	38*	14.26	–	0	0	251	53
T20	6	2	1	1*	–	100	0	0	3	1

Chapter 14

So … Who Are We?

I genuinely didn't know where this book would take me. At the outset, I knew that I had my own opinions on wicketkeeping, but I also knew that this was a book that would be led by the great wicketkeepers to whom I spoke rather than by me. So, within that dynamic I always wondered whether I would just find out things that I already knew. The question that nagged at me or even worried me a little was, 'Am I searching for further insight into wicketkeeping that doesn't actually exist?' This could have ended up being quite a boring book if the answer to that question was yes!

Well, the truth is that I had nothing to worry about. The whole experience of writing this book has turned out to be an enormous personal journey of discovery about one of my life's greatest passions. Wicketkeeping has been something that I have dedicated a huge portion of my life to, and I felt I knew a lot about it. That still holds true to some extent but the process of compiling this book has taught me so much more about it. It has helped address insecurities that I have held for years and given me perspectives into this great art within the game of cricket that I hadn't seen before. More than anything, though, it revitalised my energy and enthusiasm for wicketkeeping. As I tapped out chapters, I couldn't wait to go back and watch some of the wicketkeepers in action across world cricket right now. In short, it has reminded me how very special wicketkeeping is to me.

All the wicketkeepers that I spoke to were honest, reflective and brilliantly eloquent. I do think they felt a sense of comfort in our discussions in knowing that I was also a wicketkeeper and understood where they were coming from. It was a true honour to have the time I had with my wicketkeeping hero, Jack Russell. We delved deeply into what the art was truly about and why we did what we did. I was also able to put to bed an insecurity I have held for the last thirty years around the fact that I was often motivated by a negative thought or the thought of a negative outcome. I had always felt that because fear had played a role in my motivation, that made me average versus the best because I couldn't imagine that they could ever be driven by something negative in their minds – they were invincible, positive-thinking giants of the game! Yet, that is exactly what Jack did. His emotionalisation of the potential of a negative outcome in his mind became so powerful that it created an extraordinary level of focus to what he was doing behind the stumps. I couldn't reach the intensity within my mind that Jack did but it was a massive relief to realise that our motivations had come from the same place.

Despite having played against some of the guys for years, my chats with them made me realise how little I knew about them. To hear the resilience and determination that had driven Geraint Jones forward following the death of his mother at an early age was inspiring; and I had never known that about him. It taught me so much about him as a person and about how he had gone about his business as a wicketkeeper. Wicketkeeping just seemed to fall into his greater path of trying to overcome adversity and challenge in his life. That might well be different to every other wicketkeeper I spoke to, but it reminded me about the deep levels of resilience that exist within every wicketkeeper. We take on a relatively thankless role within cricket and the people who reach the top will be the ones who are prepared to keep beating that drum while others give up. Geraint was a personification of that.

There were certain wicketkeepers I spoke to that seemed to hold wicketkeeping on a level that, being honest, was above anything I ever did. Sarah Taylor and Keith Piper found a true home in wicketkeeping. Both have had challenges in life in trying to find peace and balance, and yet it felt like within wicketkeeping they had found a purpose that centred them. Keith's line, when he was describing the first time he kept wicket, of 'It felt like love' was incredibly powerful in making this very point. There was something about the flow and confidence that they reached when keeping that they may have struggled to achieve in other areas of life. There was something so pure about it all for them. Sarah's 'You are born to be a wicketkeeper' certainly felt very true when I think of them both.

I listen to Peter Moores probably more than anyone else in cricket and I knew that he would come up with some outstanding insights into being a wicketkeeper. The way he described how a wicketkeeper is essentially there to serve the team crystallised so much in my mind about the type of personalities wicketkeepers are and what drives them forward. Wicketkeepers see themselves as serving a greater purpose within a cricket team. They are willing to sacrifice themselves in order to help others look good and succeed. Their primary driver is based on what they believe they can offer to the team rather than what they believe they can take from the team – that in itself is very special. Michael Bates was brilliant in reflecting on his own playing career and seeing how he got so preoccupied by his perceived importance of his batting that he forgot how much he brought to the team as just a wicketkeeper, and, as a result, he never wants wicketkeepers that he now coaches to fall into that same trap. It does feel that during a time when the role of the wicketkeeper is being pulled around more than ever, that connection with what the true essence of it is all about is under threat. And that threat is not just from outside the wicketkeeping community, it is from wicketkeepers themselves: today, 'Strike Rates' seem to be the most powerful cricketing statistic, so are wicketkeepers themselves starting to forget what they can bring to a team? Without coaches like Michael Bates, quite possibly.

Chris Read surprised me a little. Although I knew him personally to some extent, I can admit that his laser focus on the efficiency of his wicketkeeping technique was not something I knew about. I thought he would be more along the lines of Sarah Taylor and Keith Piper, as a keeper who just flowed along with wicketkeeping, but there was more of a Lewis Hamilton steely intensity about him to make sure that everything he was ever doing was as efficient as possible, like the running of a Formula 1 car. Although this surprised me about him personally, it also reinforced for me that there is a powerful obsessive gene within every true wicketkeeper – Chris's was just directed at perfectly tuning the engine of his wicketkeeping! Within this we need to remember that Chris experienced a relatively dramatic change to his wicketkeeping technique mid-career, which is very unusual. As a result, the strength of his technique was always going to be a very important element within his performance. Another fascinating part of my chat with Chris was seeing how his England career ran straight into a head coach in Duncan Fletcher who was attempting to change the wicketkeeping role in his team. In some ways, the purity of Chris's approach to wicketkeeping was at odds with Duncan's motivation to see how he could push and pull that role into something different.

I must admit that I didn't plan the order in which I spoke to people for this book but I'm glad it worked out the way it did. Speaking to Jos Buttler first was excellent because it gave me the immediate insight of someone who is not necessarily seen as a 'pure' wicketkeeper. It was an opportunity to observe how much truth lay behind that perception, and, in Jos, I could see someone who was very aware of this label. In fact, he placed that label on himself. Interestingly, part of his reason for him not believing he was the purest of wicketkeepers was that if he had the choice at training to practise his batting or wicketkeeping then he would choose his batting. Yet, that is exactly what Keith Piper and Sarah Taylor said, who would both be described as 'pure' wicketkeepers. I sensed that Jos felt like he needed to admit that he was not an out-and-out wicketkeeper, but I felt that that was coming from outside comments he had heard because the more I spoke to him, the more I could see someone deeply invested in the art of wicketkeeping. He studied other keepers and analysed what worked best for him, both mentally and technically. If you combine that with his burning desire to do the job and to truly serve the interests of the team as best as you can, I'm not sure what else was missing in him to be considered a true keeper. This is an example of where I think the debate around wicketkeepers gets a little lost by casual observers. One wicketkeeper being better than another doesn't necessarily mean they are any more of a true wicketkeeper. It is just a gap in ability.

Alec Stewart, another childhood hero of mine, had the most pragmatic approach to wicketkeeping out of anyone I spoke to. For

Alec, it was a job that he had to entirely commit to in approach, practice and desire, and, importantly, he felt that was the same for all wicketkeepers. He effectively 'turned the switch on' to be a wicketkeeper and when he did that, he was all-in and became an outstanding wicketkeeper for England. He didn't necessarily buy into some of the old romanticisms about wicketkeepers and his own career was a counter to keepers having to look, sound or be born a certain way. I loved how Alec described all this because it said so much about why he was so successful in life – if he does something then he does it properly! Like Jos Buttler, if he had stepped into wicketkeeping half-heartedly then it wouldn't have worked. The reason they have survived and thrived as keepers is because they have invested themselves into it entirely. Ironically, within both their stories as perceived 'non-true' wicketkeepers, there are important lessons about what is required to be a true wicketkeeper.

What is so wonderful about this book is that every wicketkeeper I spoke to offered me something slightly different about wicketkeeping. There is something in this very point that I will come back to later in this chapter. The same applied to Warren Hegg and Amy Jones. I followed Warren's footsteps at Lancashire CCC, and I have always been a little bit in awe of him as a wicketkeeper, but I felt a real connection with him after our chat. The way Warren connected with the wicketkeeping community and what it meant to him to be a keeper was something I really identified with. It is something he still holds very dear to himself even a long time into retirement. Warren and I sit together in the history books of the wicketkeepers at Lancashire CCC, but our chat reminded me that we have a strong connection with all the keepers up and down the line of history. It is a unique community.

Amy Jones was probably the wicketkeeper I knew the least about before we spoke but her honesty and view on wicketkeeping was so refreshing. She really understood the journey that she has been and is still on as a wicketkeeper. She was crystal clear about where she had found her inspiration to develop and what that had meant for her own game. She was one of the more 'modern' wicketkeepers that I spoke to but talked about the importance of energy in a very similar way to someone like Keith Piper. And just like others, she knew that her position meant that she could impact the game significantly. She knew that she was important to a team.

So, after all this incredible insight, where did it leave me? I felt it was time for me to answer two important questions: What does it truly mean to be a wicketkeeper? And how do we decipher whether someone is a true wicketkeeper or not?

Well, as a starting point, the fact that I got something different from each person spoke volumes for how broad the wicketkeeping community is – it's not right to ever rule someone out from being a wicketkeeper. This includes physical size and technique as everyone in this book acknowledged that there has been a wide variation on this over the history of the game. Other than strength in your legs and some hand-eye coordination, there is little evidence that anything else is specifically required physically. However, there were some very strong common threads throughout all the conversations around desire, energy, attitude, focus, mindset and service to the team. Interestingly, all these things are intangibles, which points towards true wicketkeepers being a particular type of person more than anything else.

Let's quickly remind ourselves about some of the key things involved in the job of being a wicketkeeper:

1. Few people, in or out of your team, including most of the media, will really understand what is required in your job.
2. You put enormous pressure on yourself to be perfect on every single day you take to the field; and even if you do achieve perfection on a particular day, there is a chance that some people won't even notice.
3. The game will never slow down for you whether you have an injury or under any other circumstances.
4. It physically hurts – your fingers and back will never forgive you.
5. You are there to make others look good.
6. You can make a mistake and that is all anyone will remember from your day, even if the rest of the day was perfect.
7. Most people think they could 'have a go at it'.

Obviously, there is an element of humour to all these points, but they are all 100 per cent correct.

A true wicketkeeper is someone who totally and utterly dedicates themselves to every minute detail involved with the role. They understand the sacrifice, the pressure and the service and want to do it with a burning desire that moves into a full-blown obsession. The obsession will manifest itself in an endless search for perfection and the true wicketkeeper will never give up that search. Whether it be tinkering with technique, equipment, mannerisms or superstitions, all of it will be directed at achieving a day when every single ball and decision is executed with perfection. In truth, that aim will never be fully satisfied; like a nagging itch or an attempt to draw a straight line, maybe it could always be a little straighter. This sort of obsessive path will attract some quirky personalities, but it is not guaranteed. Whatever the personality trait, underlying it will be someone who's on a mission to truly master their craft; and be under no illusion – they will see it as a craft rather than a job. For some it will be a home in life, somewhere where they find meaning and purpose, like they were born to do it. But that doesn't mean they are any more worthy to be a wicketkeeper than anyone else; it is just that for them, the connection with the craft will be supremely powerful.

> When a work lifts your spirits and inspires bold and noble thoughts in you, do not look for any other standard to judge by: the work is good, the product of a master craftsman.
>
> Jean de La Bruyère

There will be some keepers for whom the skills come more naturally, but that matters little if there is not a 360 degree embrace of everything that comes with it. As the saying goes, 'Half measures will avail us nothing.' True wicketkeepers are ALL-IN. The real essence of a wicketkeeper is of someone who knows that they can impact the game significantly with their skill, energy and attitude; and they are prepared to do all of that without being noticed much. Deep down they know that they are vital to the running of the team, but they will remain humble, generous in support and a middleman or woman within team dynamics. They're able to hold a beautiful space in a game of wanting to be at the centre of the action without needing to be the centre of attention. And throughout it all, they will keep at it. Regardless of injury, loss of form or any other distraction, they will stick to their task of being a wicketkeeper. They will be entirely invested in what it means to be a wicketkeeper.

The dedicated life of a true wicketkeeper will take some maturing, like for any master craftsman. Mistakes will need to be made in order for them to grow and a balance will need to be found as how to best exert their energy on the team. Frustratingly, casual observers will likely not appreciate this but amongst wicketkeepers, they will know it. Ultimately, being the wicketkeeper in a team carries great responsibility. You are a focal point, a leader within the team whether officially or not, and a person that team dynamics will always revolve around. Like all leadership roles, sometimes people need time to grow into them. A true wicketkeeper will always understand, appreciate and honour this responsibility. They will know what they can bring to the team and why it is so important.

I discovered that in Japan, the word *takumi* refers to a craftsperson that is unrivalled in their particular field of expertise. Each *takumi* master is positioned as a team leader and is renowned for approaching their role with unrivalled passion and obsession. *Takumis* are considered the guardians of their particular artisan philosophy. I think *takumis* perfectly encapsulate what true wicketkeepers are. They also become the guardians of the art of wicketkeeping to carry forward for future generations in cricket.

Overarching everything I have said above, true wicketkeepers will know that it will be a lonely role at times and therefore their sense of community with other wicketkeepers will be the strength of a lifetime bond. They will search out fellow keepers to connect and share with as they will feel they'll be among their peers who truly understand. It truly is a brother/sisterhood.

So, forget technique, body positions, hand positions, mannerisms, size, introvert, extrovert, the way a bloody cap is positioned on a head, the essence of a true wicketkeeper is what lies in their spirit, energy, determination and honour that they bring to their role in a cricket team. If someone is ticking all these boxes, then they are true wicketkeeper. The next time you hear someone questioning the validity of someone as a wicketkeeper because of their skill level at that time or their physical look then remember everything within this book. The true judgement of a wicketkeeper lies with what's inside them rather than any outside appearance. If they are utterly dedicated to their path ahead then that should be respected above all else.

Some people will never understand what it means to be a wicketkeeper and, as frustrating as that is, that's OK, because part of the true essence of a being wicketkeeper is to accept that and carry on regardless. Granted, as a former professional wicketkeeper, I could rightfully be accused of bias but my opinion is that wicketkeepers are the great servants of the game and therefore hold a special place within it. I feel honoured to be part of this group of cricketers.

It takes a particular type of person to be a true wicketkeeper and in my eyes they are all heroes of the beautiful game of cricket.

Long live the wicketkeeper!

Acknowledgements

Jo – thank you for your undying love and support, which gives me the freedom to do so much in my life, including writing. I love you today, tomorrow, and always.

Jonathan Wright – your faith in me to write has given me one of my great joys in life and I will be forever grateful to you for that.

Jos Buttler – you are an inspiration for how all professional sportspeople should conduct themselves. You are a great of our game but carry yourself with amazing grace and humility.

Geraint Jones – I wish I had known more about your story previously. You're a good man who deserves everything you earn in life.

Chris Read – your dedication to our art is a shining example for all young wicketkeepers out there. If future keepers follow your path, we are going to produce many brilliant ones.

Sarah Taylor – thank you for letting me into your world. You will rightfully be remembered as one of England's greatest-ever wicketkeepers.

Jack Russell – the Wicketkeeping King. You inspired me and so many others. Our chat for this book will live long in my memory.

Alec Stewart – the cricketer that I wished I could have been; you are a true legend of the game, and a gentleman to go with it.

Amy Jones – your path as a wicketkeeper is a great example of the life we lead. Continue to blossom and inspire others to follow you.

Michael Bates – wicketkeepers across our county will be lucky to be coached by you. You are passing on the precious values of what it means to be a true wicketkeeper.

Keith Piper – you were a wicketkeeping genius. Thank you for giving me your time and insight; it should be heard more.